The Fall of the House of Percy, 1368–1408

The Fall of the House of Percy, 1368–1408

RICHARD LOMAS

JOHN DONALD

First published in Great Britain in 2007 by
John Donald, an imprint of Birlinn Ltd

West Newington House
10 Newington Road
Edinburgh
EH9 1QS

www.birlinn.co.uk

ISBN 10: 0 85976 647 0
ISBN 13: 978 0 85976 647 0

British Library Cataloguing-in-Publication Data
A catalogue record for this book is available on request from the British Library

Typeset by Hewer Text UK Ltd, Edinburgh
Printed and bound in Great Britain by Athenaeum Press, Gateshead

To Joan, whose support and help have been invaluable, and my Alnwick friends, particularly the late Marjorie Deakin

Contents

Plates

Plates

Maps

Genealogical tables

Preface

The deposition (in 1399) and subsequent murder (in 1400) of Richard II were not unprecedented events. Three-quarters of a century earlier, in 1327, Richard's great grandfather, Edward II, suffered the same fate. But between these two episodes, seemingly so similar, there were significant differences. Edward II was not murdered by his successor or to secure the succession. His successor was his eldest son, Edward III, who had no part in his father's death and whose claim to the throne was undeniable. In contrast, Richard II was deposed by his cousin, Henry of Bolingbroke, who replaced him on the throne, his right to which was open to question. Although Edward III gained from the crime, he was not the author of it; Henry IV, on the other hand, committed the crime from which he directly and intentionally benefited.

Because of these differences, Richard II's deposition and murder reverberated throughout the fifteenth century and lay at the heart of many of the violent political conflicts that bedevilled much of that century. It is not surprising that Shakespeare made his tragedy *Richard II* and what he saw as flowing from it the matter of no fewer than seven plays, almost a fifth of his dramatic output. And it did not take Shakespeare to elicit from Elizabeth I the remark 'Know ye not that I am Richard II?'. What happened in 1399 and 1400 was a standing reminder that being the Lord's anointed was ultimately no guarantee of protection from dire political misfortune.

Shakespeare's plays about Richard II and Henry IV have remained popular and frequently produced down to our own time, when the events with which they deal have received considerable attention from modern historians. The three royal characters – Richard II, Henry IV and his father, John of Gaunt, Duke of Lancaster – have been the subject of seven full-length studies, encompassing ten volumes by, respectively, Henri

Wallon, Anthony Steel and Nigel Saul; J.H. Wylie and J.L. Kirby; and Sydney Armitage Smith and Anthony Goodman, as well as almost countless articles on individual aspects, incidents and facets by a large number of historians. Indeed, it is not unfair to say that Richard II has been done to death in both senses of that term.

There is, however, one aspect that will bear further consideration. Central and crucial in the downfall of Richard II and the success of Henry IV were three members of a non-royal magnate family: Henry Percy, created Earl of Northumberland in 1377; his brother, Sir Thomas Percy, made Earl of Worcester in 1397; and his eldest son, Sir Henry Percy, better known by his sobriquet, 'Hotspur'. Many of the actions of the Earl and Hotspur (but not of Thomas Percy) have been the subjects of detailed study by Anthony Tuck, J.W.M. Bean and particularly Peter McNiven. But they are narrow in their focus and their findings, arguments and conclusions are published in academic journals normally visited only by professional historians. The aim of this book is to integrate into a coherent account, and for a broad readership, what they and others have discovered about these men, so as to clarify, as far as is at present possible, how they enhanced their wealth and to explain their ambitions and actions in the political and military events in which they were involved. The period covered is the forty years between the last years of Edward III's reign and the catastrophe they brought upon themselves in the first decade of the fifteenth century. If the timescale is narrow, the geographical spread is not, since they were involved in matters of major consequence in England, Scotland and Wales and in much of Western Europe.

'As far as is at present possible' is the operative term. Students of any political aspect of this period are obliged to study, as well as state records, contemporary or near contemporary narrative sources. However, consulting these is to be driven to agreement with G.O. Sayles' cry of exasperation that 'nothing is more futile than the attempt to wring the truth from these narratives, based as they are upon gossip, news-letters and propaganda'. The validity of this is amply underscored and given considerable definition in Louisa Duls' categorisation and analysis of the chronicles that record in varying degrees of detail the events of some or all of this period. She made clear that all of them are to some extent partial, in both senses of that word, and none deals in complete detail with all of the various episodes. The frustrating inability of these sources to yield the truth has been confirmed more recently by Chris Given-Wilson. And, in a microscopic way, the danger of relying on the chroniclers' tales is neatly and effectively illustrated by Harriet Hansen's study of the events of 15 June 1381 at Smithfield.

Any account or explanation of any incident or aspect is therefore a choice between accepting one version or using several to arrive at a conclusion that makes inherent sense. The former would simply endorse the partiality of the chosen account; the latter leads to statements that are possibilities, not certainties. This, I believe, is unavoidable. In considering the evidence and forming opinions, I have leant towards the cynical view and have been reluctant to give any of the characters the benefit of the moral doubt. Despite their adherence to the precepts of knightly honour and loyalty to the Crown, the reality was that the political game was played with increasing ruthlessness: to lose was to die. It would be naïve to think that the men of the time were not conscious of this and that they knew that their deeds had to be at odds with their words. Before looking at these three men, however, some account of the rise of their family to prominence in the fourteenth century is necessary.

Two further points of explanation are required. One is that, like most magnate families, the Percys had a fixed naming pattern for their sons. The heir-apparent was always named Henry; the next son was called Thomas; and the third, if there was one, Ralph. This pattern, which was maintained from the mid-thirteenth until the late sixteenth century, while suiting their purposes, makes for confusion. In the hope of obviating this, I shall normally refer to Henry, First Earl of Northumberland, as 'the Earl'; to his son, also Henry, as 'Hotspur'; and to the Earl's younger brother as 'Thomas Percy', even though he too became an earl. The other is the use of 'Percys' rather than 'Percies': the reason is that this is the spelling preferred by the present members of the family.

ONE

The Percy Family Before 1368

The progenitor of the Percy family was William de Percy I, who acquired the nickname '*al gernons*' ('with the whiskers'). Although his career in England can be reconstructed in brief outline, his origin will probably continue to be a matter of speculation. Given that he was active in England in a responsible role shortly after 1066, and that he lived until 1099, it is likely that he was born in the 1030s; and in the light of the family's early name sequence, it is possible that his father's name was Alan. Where he came from can be narrowed down to one of two places in Normandy. One is the village of Percy in the *département* of La Manche, about nineteen miles west of Avranches. The alternative is the village of Percy en Auge in the *département* of Calvados, about fifteen miles south-east of Caen in the valley of the River Dives. Earlier opinion favoured the former, but such evidence as there is, and it is very slight, suggests that the latter has the better claim. Whatever the truth, it is probable that he was not out of the topmost drawer of Norman society. Also uncertain is when he arrived in England. I believe Edward de Fonblanque was right to doubt his presence in the Conqueror's army that landed in Sussex in late September 1066 and to incline to the following year, 1067.

What is certain is that he arrived in England in time to play a major part in the brutal suppression of the native revolts in Yorkshire in the years 1068–70, and to be a member of the Conqueror's expedition into Scotland in 1072 that secured the submission of Malcolm III at Abernethy. Almost no detail of this has survived, but his appointment in 1069 as Castellan of York and deputy to the Sheriff of Yorkshire, Hugh Fitz Baldric, points to military competence and to the Conqueror's confidence in his loyalty. This confidence was not misplaced: there is no evidence that Percy was involved in any of the rebellions against the Conqueror, and he appears as

1

a witness on many royal charters issued by the king at places as far apart as Lincoln and Hastings.

This suggests a peripatetic existence. In fact, Percy appears to have spent a fair amount of time in Yorkshire, where most of the property he acquired was located. This impression is reinforced by his involvement in the restarting of monastic life at the site of the famous Anglo-Saxon monastery at Whitby through his support for a man named Reinfrid, who probably had been one of his knights and who had retired from military life to become a monk at Evesham. From there he came north in 1074 with Aldwin, the prior of the neighbouring monastery of Winchcombe, who, with the blessing of Walcher, the Bishop of Durham, restarted monastic life at Jarrow and Wearmouth. Reinfrid, however, soon moved to Whitby, the ruins of which he had seen during his fighting days. The development of Whitby was held up by the opposition of a certain Stephen of Whitby, whose ideas of what a monastery should be were seriously at odds with those of Reinfrid and Percy. It was not until the death of the Conqueror, who had favoured Stephen, that Percy was able to develop Whitby in accordance with his own ideas. These were distinctly old fashioned and out of line with those launched in the third quarter of the eleventh century by Popes Leo IX (1049–54) and Gregory VII (1073–85), which demanded that the Church at all levels be free of lay control. In contrast to this new doctrine, although a layman, he invested himself with the post of abbot, appointing his brother, Serlo, also a layman, to be in charge on the spot as prior. To Percy, what he endowed remained his: Whitby was his monastery and it existed for the benefit of himself and his family.

If Percy was out of sympathy with the reformist ideas taking hold in ecclesiastical circles throughout Europe in the late eleventh century, he was not impervious to the call of Pope Urban II in 1096 for a concerted effort to rescue the sites of Christ's life and ministry in the Holy Land from Turkish/Islamic control. Although by this date an old man, he joined the First Crusade and, unlike so many on that expedition, he made it to Jerusalem. However, he died on Mount Joy, overlooking the city, prior to the appalling massacre committed by the crusading army.

William de Percy I was succeeded by his son, Alan, the product of his marriage to Emma, daughter of Hugh de Port en Bessin, the lord of Basing in Hampshire. Hugh's origins were in the same part of Normandy as Percy en Auge, which may help to confirm this as the Percy home. Alan's headship of the family coincided almost exactly with the reign of Henry I (1100–35). Like his father, Alan was loyal to the Crown and as a consequence prospered. He became involved in Scottish affairs, but only to a limited extent and, as a result, unlike a number of northern barons, he acquired little property north of the Border. He married Emma, daughter of a fellow Yorkshire baron, Gilbert de Gant (Ghent) and they are known to have had at least four sons, the eldest of whom was William, presumably named after his grandfather.

William de Percy II inherited from his father on the latter's death, which occurred sometime between 1131 and 1135. He too maintained what was by now a family tradition of loyalty to the Crown. This was most clearly demonstrated in 1138 when, unlike several northern barons, he fought in the English army assembled by Thurstan, the Archbishop of York, that repulsed the invasion of David I of Scotland at Cowton Moor, near Northallerton. He was also an active promoter of the new forms of monasticism that became hugely popular in his lifetime. He was responsible for founding the Cistercian abbey at Sallay (now Sawley) in the Craven district of West Yorkshire and the small nunnery at Stainfield near Lincoln; also he assisted his daughter Agnes and her husband in their support of the Gilbertine house at Sixhills near Market Rasen, also in Lincolnshire.

William de Percy II died between Easter 1174 and Easter 1175, and with his death there began a major crisis in the family's history that was to last for seventy years. He had married twice, first Alice de Tonbridge, and in 1166 after her death, Sibil, the widow of another Yorkshire baron, Robert de Ros, Lord of Helmsley. Despite this, his only surviving children were two daughters, his only son, Alan, having predeceased him. The elder girl, Matilda, married William de Newburgh, Earl of Warwick. It was fortunate for the family's survival that this marriage was childless, and that after her husband's death in 1184, she paid King Henry II a considerable sum of money to retain her portion of the Percy estate and to remain a widow. Her widowhood was long, lasting until 1203 or 1204, but her decision

3

ensured that, barring accidents, on her death the property would continue in Percy ownership.

Much, however, would depend upon what happened to her sister, Agnes, who married Jocelin, Count of Louvain (Leuven), son of Godfrey, Duke of Lower Lorraine. Jocelin's presence in England was due to the marriage in 1121 of his half-sister, Adeliza, to Henry I. Adeliza was Henry's second wife, his first wife, Matilda, having died in 1118. He might not have remarried had it not been for the death in 1120 of his only legitimate son, William, in a shipping disaster off Barfleur. Given that Henry is reputed to have sired numerous illegitimate children, it is curious that his second marriage proved to be barren, the more so since Adeliza was young and by her second husband, William d'Albini, whom she married in 1138 three years after Henry's death, she had several children.

It is likely that Agnes de Percy's marriage to Jocelin de Louvain took place shortly after Adeliza's own second marriage, since she gave as a wedding gift to Agnes and Jocelin a very substantial estate centred on Petworth in Sussex. Unlike that of her sister, Agnes's marriage proved fruitful: she and Jocelin are known to have had eight children, including two sons, Henry and Richard, who survived to manhood. Significantly, both adopted the name Percy. Here there is a problem, however. Traditionally, Henry was thought to be the elder, but M.J. Vine has argued that Richard was the senior by ten years. If so, he was the heir presumptive to the entire estate, following the death of his father in 1184. Agnes, however, like her sister, had a long widowhood, surviving until 1202.

Both brothers married. Henry's wife was Isabel, daughter of another Yorkshire baron, Adam de Brus, Lord of Skelton, by whom he had a son, William. But in 1198, shortly after William's birth, Henry died. His widow married again, her second husband being a Northumberland man, Sir Roger Mauduit. The wardship of the infant William, however, was granted to William Brewer, a man close to King John, who married him to his daughter, Joan. In contrast, Richard de Percy had a long life, outliving his brother by forty-six years, not dying until 1244. Although twice married, he left no surviving children, and consequently his sole heir was his nephew, William. By these fortuitous developments the fission of

4

the estate arising from William de Percy II's failure to produce a male heir was repaired after an interlude of seventy years. While both uncle and nephew were alive, however, there was bad blood between them arising from the division of the estate. Not surprisingly, therefore, they took opposing sides in the quarrel between King John and a section of the baronage. William, the nephew, who married the daughter of one of the king's leading supporters, remained loyal; Richard, the uncle, was a prominent member of the opposition and was one of the twenty-five barons charged with enforcing the arrangements prescribed by Magna Carta.

William de Percy III did not long enjoy his inheritance since he died the following year, 1245. By his first wife, Joan Brewer, he had only daughters. Consequently, after her death, which occurred before 1233, he remarried. His second wife, Ellen, daughter of Ingram de Balliol, began the long-lasting association of the Percy family with Scotland. Ellen was more successful than her predecessor, producing four sons. It was the eldest of these, Henry, who at the age of ten succeeded his father in 1245. Henry de Percy II had a short life, dying in 1272 at the age of thirty-seven. He was involved in the political upheavals and civil wars of the 1260s, initially supporting Simon de Montfort, but then returning to the side of the Crown. Consequently, he escaped unscathed, although this may have been in part due to his association with John de Warenne, Earl of Surrey, a powerful man and a leading royalist, whose daughter, Eleanor, he married.

At the time of Henry de Percy II's death his family had been in England for a little over two hundred years. They had rapidly attained the level of wealth that qualified them to be regarded as substantial members of the baronage. But they were some way short of the top stratum of English society. Moreover, as will become more apparent when their estate is analysed, they were essentially a northern family, and more particularly a Yorkshire family, a fact underlined by several of their marriages. In the next hundred years this was to change, so that by the late fourteenth century the Percy family had become one of the wealthiest and most powerful of the English nobility, with links with the royal family. The man responsible for initiating this expansion was Henry de Percy III, the younger son of Henry de Percy II. His beginnings were not auspicious: he was born posthumously, seven months after his father's death. Moreover, he had an elder brother, John, born in 1270, about whom little is known, not even the date of his death, except that this took place sometime between June 1285 and July 1293. It seems unlikely that John married or, if he did, he had no children, since his successor was his younger brother, Henry.

Henry de Percy III had an outstanding career as a soldier. By the time he had reached his majority in 1294, he appears already to have gained a reputation as a warrior and to have shown great potential as a commander. Military matters being his bent and his talent, he was fortunate in coming of age on the eve of the long Anglo-Scottish war. In its first phase, when fighting was all but continuous, Percy rapidly proved to be one of the most able of a group of young captains discovered by Edward I. His military career lasted twenty-one years and ended with his death in October 1314, a few weeks after the Battle of Bannockburn. The fact that he was not present at this battle suggests that he may have terminally ill by that summer, since it is almost inconceivable that, had he been fit, he would not have been part of Edward II's huge army assembled to attempt to lift the siege of Stirling.

Why men like Percy were prepared to devote their lives to war in Scotland is to be largely explained by the prospect of gain, and in particular the hope of acquiring estates of landowners who lost out through their support for the Scottish king. These gains were to be of short duration, although this could not have been known at the time. Percy was one of the major beneficiaries. In 1299, he was granted the estates of Ingram de Balliol, to whom he was related, in Kirkcudbrightshire and Angus, and in 1304 he was given the earldom of Buchan with its huge estate in north-eastern Scotland. His possession lasted only two years before it was regranted to its original owner when he renewed his allegiance to Edward I. In compensation, Percy was granted the earldom of Carrick, confiscated from Robert Bruce following his rebellion in 1306. Grants such as these were both rewards for services already rendered and incentives to their new owners to commit themselves permanently to the king's struggle to subjugate Scotland.

Another indicator of his rising fortunes was the award in 1299 of the title 'Lord Percy', which coincided with his marriage to Eleanor Fitzalan, a close relation, perhaps a daughter, of Richard Fitzalan, Earl of Arundel. He was a nobleman of the first rank and the dominant landowner in Sussex where Percy had his Petworth estate. This match may explain Percy's decision to change his coat armour. Previously these had been *azure, a fess engrailed of five fusils or* (five gold lozenges or fusils on a blue ground). These he replaced with *or, a lion rampant azure* (a blue lion rampant on a gold ground), identical to those of Fitzalan, except for the tinctures (colours). Her splendid tomb near the high altar of Beverley Minster proclaims Eleanor Fitzalan's high status. On the other hand, it has been argued that Percy simply adopted without any change the arms of the Redvers family, Earls of Devon, that had become extinct in 1262 and that he did so because of their common ancestor, the pre-Conquest lords of Vernon in Normandy.

If most of the Percy gains in Scotland proved to be temporary, those in Northumberland did not. Their rise to dominance in that county began with First Lord Percy's acquisition of Alnwick in 1309, an event thoroughly explored by J.M.W. Bean. His motive, Bean argues, was the need for a property half way between his Yorkshire estates and his newly acquired possessions in Scotland. This may have been so, but the **barony** was well worth having in its own right. It was the largest of the twenty baronies created in Northumberland between 1095 and 1135 following the suppression of the earldom of Northumbria by King William II. From the mid-twelfth century it descended in the family of de Vesci until the death of William de Vesci in July 1297. As a result of the death of his son, John, in May 1295, he had no legitimate heir and in consequence devised a settlement for the disposal of his estate after his death. This involved granting all of it to the Bishop of Durham, Anthony Bek, who reinvested him with it for life with two **remainders**, assuming his death without legitimate heirs, which was virtually certain. His lands in Yorkshire and Lincolnshire were to go to his illegitimate son, William de Vesci, known as William de Vesci of Kildare on account of his successful career in Ireland. The Northumberland property, however, was to remain with Bishop Bek. Upon de Vesci's death, this settlement came into force.

The 1297 arrangements remained in place until 1309, when Bek sold Alnwick to Henry, First Lord Percy. The purchase price is not known, but is thought to have been between 4,000 **marks** (£2,666.67) and 10,000 marks (£6,666.67), and certainly large enough to have made it necessary for Percy to borrow from Italian bankers. This, however, was not the end of the story, for a suspicion began to circulate that the transaction was not entirely licit in that Bek was not really the owner but a trustee holding the property for a future legitimate member of the de Vesci family. The issue did not become a live one until the early 1320s, by which time Henry, First Lord Percy, and William de Vesci of Kildare were dead, the latter killed at Bannockburn. The occasion of the challenge to Percy ownership appears to have been the coming of age of Henry, Second Lord Percy, in 1321. The challenger was Gilbert de Aton (East Ayton near Scarborough), who was proved by **inquests** held in 1314 and 1315 to be the nearest legitimate male heir of William de Vesci and in consequence secured possession of the Vesci lands in Yorkshire and Lincolnshire in 1317. The upshot was that in 1323 Henry, Second Lord Percy agreed to pay Gilbert de Aton the sum of 700 marks (£466.67) for his confirmation of Bishop Bek's sale of Alnwick to Percy's father. In the end, only half the agreed sum was paid, but it does suggest that Percy was not sufficiently certain of his ground to risk court action, and that de Aton was prepared to settle out of court for the same reason, and also perhaps because he feared to take on such a powerful adversary. Whatever the reasons, the Percys retained Alnwick.

In addition to making Percy possession of Alnwick legally secure, the Second Lord Percy increased his stake in Northumberland with the acquisition of two other baronies. The first was Warkworth, granted to him in 1332. This was the consequence of an agreement made with the Crown five years earlier to defend the eastern Border for an annual fee of £500. At the Crown's request, Percy agreed to relinquish this in return for Warkworth, at that time belonging to Sir John Clavering and **entailed** on his male heirs. However, as he was old and had no heir, when he died in 1332 the barony **escheated** to the Crown, which immediately invested Percy with it. For Percy the bargain was a good one since the contract fee, although substantial, was unlikely to be permanent, while Warkworth would be held by him and his descendants in perpetuity. The Crown also benefited in that it was relieved of the difficult task of finding a large sum of money every year. The second baronial acquisition was Beanley, which had belonged to the Scottish Earls of Dunbar since its grant to Gospatric, Earl of Dunbar by Henry I. One of the consequences of the war was the disappearance of the cross-Border estate, which neither king was prepared to tolerate. Magnates in both countries had to decide to which Crown they would give their allegiance and to suffer the loss of their estates in the other realm. In 1335, Patrick, Earl of Dunbar opted to be a Scot and consequently forfeited Beanley, which was immediately granted to Percy.

Percy also made gains in Scotland during the 1330s. In July 1333, Edward Balliol, then briefly King of Scotland, granted him the Bruce estates in Annandale and Moffatdale. But a more powerful English magnate, Edward de Bohun, Earl of Hereford, laid claim to them under the terms of grant made to his father in 1306. Percy agreed to Edward III's request to relinquish them in return for Jedburgh and Jed Forest in Roxburghshire, the constableship of Berwick Castle and an annual fee of 500 marks (£333.34) from the customs revenue of Berwick. Percy possession of Jedburgh was of longer duration than that of their other Scottish acquisitions, lasting until the early years of the next century. It also became the cause of the classic cross-Border feud between the Percy and Douglas families since Jedburgh and Jed Forest had been granted by Robert I to Sir William Douglas during the 1320s. The property was too valuable for either family to relinquish without a struggle.

Also, between 1343 and 1350 Percy purchased properties in four important **boroughs** close to his areas of interest. Perhaps the most significant was the **messuage** in London in Aldersgate in the parish of St Agnes that he acquired in May 1343 from the Dean of St Paul's Cathedral. Its purpose was not to increase his rent roll, but to be a residence near Westminster for use when Parliament met there and generally to be a base close to the seat of government. The following year, he purchased two tenements in Walmgate in the parish of St Denis in York and about the same time a messuage in Beverley, the nearest town to his East Riding **manor** house at Leconfield. The York property was specifically said to be for his residence when in the city. Lastly, in February 1350, he bought from John Pulhore, Rector of Whickham in County Durham, a messuage on Pilgrim Street in Newcastle upon Tyne.

Percy married Idonea de Clifford, the daughter of one of his father's companions in arms, Robert, Lord Clifford, perhaps the ablest captain of his generation, who was killed at Bannockburn. He too gained from the wars in the form of a grant in 1306 of Robert Bruce's estate around Hartlepool in County Durham. The centre of his power, however, was Brougham in Westmorland, from where he was able to exert influence on the western Border. An alliance between these two families was in their common interest and was strategically sensible.

The marriage of the Second Lord Percy and Idonea de Clifford was fruitful, including three sons and three daughters. The eldest son, also named Henry, succeeded on his father's death in February 1352 as the Third Lord Percy. Like his father and grandfather, his was a largely military career, although much of it was spent in France rather than Scotland. The underlying reason for this was the English victory at Neville's Cross in October 1346, which gave England control of the Scottish border counties and in which the Second Lord Percy played a notable part. Furthermore, the Scottish king, David II, was captured after the battle and remained a prisoner in England for eleven years. These developments combined to make the Border a relatively quiet place: for a man of martial inclination the place to be was France.

Perhaps the most significant event in the Third Lord Percy's life was his marriage to Mary, daughter of Henry of Grosmont, Earl (and from 1351 Duke) of Lancaster, the greatest of Edward III's captains, who made an outstanding contribution to English military success during the earliest phase of the Hundred Years War. Lancaster would have known Percy through their mutual involvement in the war, which almost certainly explains their agreement to link their families by marriage. Its importance, however, lay in the person of the bride's father: Henry of Grosmont was the grandson of Edmund, nicknamed 'Crouchback', the second son of Henry III. Both the Second Lord Percy and the Third Lord Percy married a daughter of one of their comrades in arms, but there the similarity ends. While the Second Lord Percy's wife was the daughter of a rising northern baron, the Third Lord Percy espoused a member of the royal family, albeit one on its outer fringes. The contrast underlines the rising standing of the Percy family.

The wealth and status of a magnate family were based upon land. It is therefore important to look in more detail at the portfolio of properties the Percys built up in the three centuries after their arrival in England. The foundation was laid by William de Percy I, to whom the Conqueror granted an extensive estate in Yorkshire as a reward for his part in the suppression of native resistance. Paul Dalton's detailed study of the Norman settlement of Yorkshire shows that by the time of the Domesday Survey of 1085 the Percy barony was the seventh largest of the twenty-five created in that county. It comprised seventy-seven manors and seven **berewicks** (discrete farms), and was reckoned to amount to 303 **carucates**. As the carucate was a unit of assessment for taxation and other obligations, it had no standard size; consequently, it is all but impossible to arrive at an accurate acreage. Virtually all incomers settled by the Conqueror on confiscated English estates built castles for security and control and as centres of estate administration. Percy was no exception, his being sited at Topcliffe, Spofforth and Tadcaster, all close to each other and to York. The estate was augmented during the reign of William II, notably by the manors of Catton and Whitby, formerly belonging to Hugh de Avranches, Earl of Chester. Almost certainly they were a reward for Percy's loyalty during the rebellion of 1088.

Alan de Percy acquired further properties from the Crown. Again, loyalty, in his case to Henry I during the uncertain early years of his reign, was the likely reason. The most important of them was half the far western region of Yorkshire known as Cravenshire, which had been confiscated from its previous tenant, Roger le Poitevin. The bulk of this property was in the Ribble Valley and was centred on the castle at Gisburn, which may have been built by him or perhaps by his predecessor. Alan also acquired land in the vicinity of Tadcaster and the manor of Upleatham near the Tees. In all, Alan de Percy increased the size of the estate by 179 carucates.

Many of these properties were not retained in hand but created into feudal tenancies. The Domesday Survey shows William de Percy I to have disposed of thirty-two manors and three berewicks in creating seventeen knights' fees, which accounted for just under half of the carucates he had been given. By 1135, that is, at the time of Alan de Percy's death, the number of knights' fees on the estate had risen to twenty-three, and by 1166 it was probably fifty. This increase may have been due to the increase in the size of the estate but also to the need to trade land for loyalty, especially during the difficult days of Stephen's reign. Unfortunately, it is not possible to discern how the estate was organised at this date.

Also in the first two generations, the Percys acquired a relatively small estate in the Lindsey district of Lincolnshire. In the early fourteenth century, there was no **demesne**. The land, which amounted to nearly sixty-three carucates in nineteen townships, was divided between four whole and ten fractional knights' fees, of which one whole and two half fees belonged to three religious houses. At an early date they also possessed the manor of Hambledon between Godalming and Haslemere in Surrey. It had been granted to William de Percy I by his father-in-law, Hugh de Port, on the occasion of Percy's marriage to his daughter, Emma. But it was lost to the estate in the middle years of the twelfth century, when Jocelin de Louvain gave it to his elder daughter, Eleanor.

Hambledon was not far from the main Percy interest in the south, the estate at Petworth. This amounted to a quarter of the lordship of Arundel that was forfeited by Robert of Belleme, because of his support for Robert, Duke of Normandy, who invaded England in 1102 with the aim of supplanting his younger brother, Henry I. The Arundel lordship was one of the properties with which Henry I endowed his second wife, Adeliza, with the proviso that it and the other properties given to her should be permanently alienated to her. Adeliza, therefore, was within her rights in bestowing Petworth on her brother and his wife, Agnes de Percy. Four-teenth-century evidence shows that the Percys retained Petworth itself and the nearby townships of Sutton and Duncton in demesne. The remainder of the estate, covering property in nineteen places in Sussex, comprised nine feudal tenancies rated at twenty-two knights' fees, which was the original feudal obligation. The Petworth estate was not a tenancy in chief but held of the lordship of Arundel.

Thereafter, the estate remained basically static until the early fourteenth century, although not entirely so, since marriages brought with them some important additions. The Percy Cartulary, compiled in the late fourteenth century, records that in the 1190s Peter de Brus granted to Henry de Percy I the manor of Kirklevington in the North Riding, except for the service of four free tenants, with his sister, Isabel. In the following generation, the two marriages of William de Percy III brought notable gains: by the first, to Joan Brewer, he acquired Foston in Leicestershire, and by the second, to Ellen de Balliol, Dalton Piercy in County Durham. Neither property was destined to be a permanent accretion: Dalton was sold to Sir John Neville of Raby in 1370; and Foston was lost at the forfeiture of the Third Earl of Northumberland in 1462.

In addition to these windfalls, gains were made as the result of a policy aimed at buying out small free tenants, particularly in the demesne manors. For example, the Percy Cartulary includes no fewer than thirty documents relating to the transfer of land in Leconfield, near Beverley in the East Riding of Yorkshire, from a local family called Agillum to Richard de Percy. In this case, the transactions were in effect mortgage foreclosures. In another case involving Richard de Percy, a John de Beauver made over to him nine bovates in Foston in the North Riding of Yorkshire, six in demesne and three in the hands of tenants, in return for 15 marks which Beauver needed to discharge a debt to Jewish money-lenders. In most cases, however, the circumstances of the transaction were not recorded.

Then, in a twenty-five year period in the early fourteenth century, the estate was expanded considerably in a northwards direction. The first and most important acquisition, purchased by Henry, First Lord Percy in 1309, was the barony of Alnwick in Northumberland, for which the service of ten knights was owed to the Crown. Its core comprised nine demesne townships, two of which, Alnwick and its nearby port of Alnmouth, had borough status. The others were Denwick (which was regarded as an adjunct of Alnwick), Lesbury, Longhoughton, Tughall, Swinhoe, Chatton and Alnham. In addition, there were twenty-two feudal tenants who between them held thirty-three other townships. Their combined service amounted to just under twenty-one knights' fees, which carried the additional obligation of castle guard at Alnwick. Henry,

First Lord Percy also made an important acquisition in Yorkshire. This was the manor of Pocklington in the East Riding of Yorkshire, which he secured at the end of 1302 from the Cistercian abbey of Meaux in exchange for the advowson of the parish church of Nafferton and an acre of land there.

His son added even more. In 1328, he acquired the barony of Warkworth from the Crown. Although smaller in size than Alnwick, most of it was demesne. Its most important constituents were the ancient boroughs of Warkworth, Corbridge and Rothbury and its satellite, Newtown, while Newburn, which included the hamlets of Wallbottle and Butterlaw, had been classified as a borough at an earlier date. The other members were Birling, Acklington, Thropton and Snitter. The only place not under direct control was Throckley, an ancient **drengage** that had been reclassified as a **socage** tenement by 1242. In contrast, the barony of Beanley, secured in 1335, had almost no demesne. Originally it was not a barony but a grand **sergeanty**, whose first holder, Gospatric, was charged not with military service but with brokering cross-Border disputes, a task he was well fitted to undertake in that he had land in both kingdoms and was closely related to both royal houses. Beanley's original status meant that none of its free tenants owed knight service. Beanley and Shipley were rent-paying socage tenements; a third holding comprising six townships owed 6d (2p) or a sparrow hawk; while another comprising four townships was held in return for providing hospitality. A further five townships were had come through marriage and one belonged to a religious house. Henry, Second Lord Percy also reinforced his title to the Northumberland manor of Thirston, but only after a dispute. A member of the barony of Mitford, this manor was purchased in 1275 by John de Vesci. Forty years later, the lordship of Mitford barony was vested in Aymer de Valence, Earl of Pembroke. He died in 1324, but it was not until 1331 that an inquest confirmed that Pembroke had not been in possession of Thirston on the day he died and that therefore Percy was its rightful owner.

What was the estate worth annually? With the exception of a handful relating to the Sussex properties, virtually all the fourteenth-century estate administration documents have been lost. Consequently, the only evi-

14

dence available is that contained in the inquests *post mortem*. These provide only a notional indication of gross value and also may be deficient in that portions of an estate were in the hands of dowagers and the heir if he was of full age and married. Inquests relating to the deaths of the First Lord Percy in 1314, the Second Lord Percy in 1352 and the Third Lord Percy in 1368 are extant. All are useful, but it is unfortunate that there is a membrane missing from the latest of them, that of 1368. The only estate managers' accounts available are those relating to the Sussex demesne townships in the years 1347–53. These reveal an annual income of nearly £238, the bulk of which came from the sale of produce (the demesne was still being worked directly) and tenant rents. Expenses amounted to £90, thereby lowering net income to £148, that is, to 62 per cent of the gross total.

The Yorkshire properties were far more extensive and of greater value. The best of the inquests *post mortem*, that of 1353, records ten demesne manors: Spofforth, Tadcaster and Cleatop in the West Riding; Topcliffe, Catton and Kirklevington in the North Riding; Nafferton, Leconfield, Seamer and Pocklington in the East Riding. It does not mention Gisburn in Cravenshire and that the yield from two manors was minimal since they were in the hands of the heir and his wife. In addition there were sixty-eight knights' fees, almost all fragmented, with elements in 126 places. The deficiencies of this and the other inquests *post mortem* means that their total annual value cannot be calculated with certainty, but it was definitely in excess of £400 and it is reasonable to think that it was probably close to £500.

The Lincolnshire properties were not included in the 1353 inquest because they had been assigned to the Rector of Spofforth in 1345. In 1368, however, they were reckoned to be worth £8 a year, comprising rents from the small religious houses at Sixhills, Thornton and Elsham, in addition to seven fractional knights' fees.

For Northumberland, the 1368 inquest shows that, although roughly equal in size as regards their demesne element, the baronies of Alnwick and Warkworth were not equal in value. The annual worth of Alnwick's nine demesne townships was said to be £187. The largest element was tenant rents, which produced £102; the demesne lands, which were

15

rented, yielded £40; and the manorial appurtenances, such as mills and including court income, netted £46. In addition, the obligation of castle guard, incumbent on all the twenty-two feudal tenants of the barony (whose combined service amounted to just short of twenty knights' fees) was by this date commuted to fixed annual payments amounting to £13 6s 5d (£13.32). This raised the annual value of the barony to just over £200.

This was less than half the value assigned in 1289 on the death of John de Vesci, when the sum recorded was £466 11s 11½d (£466.60). Between the two dates the value of the demesne at Alnwick dropped from just short of £7 to barely over £4 and the income from the burgage and freehold tenants of the borough fell catastrophically from £61 to little more than £11. Throughout the barony there were 123 **bondlands**. In 1289, their annual rent was £1 6s 8d (£1.34) a year; in 1368 the rent was half that sum and only 84½ were fully tenanted, the remainder being described as waste, although they did yield some income in the form of herbage rents. The prime cause of this decline was almost certainly falling population due to plague. The other possible cause, Scottish raids, was probably of only marginal significance, since in 1368 the county had enjoyed around twenty relatively peaceful years, thanks to the defeat of the Scottish army at Neville's Cross in 1346 and the consequent English control of the Scottish border districts.

The value of Warkworth barony was a fifth larger than that of Alnwick: just over £257: Warkworth Manor £70 9s 10d (£70.49); Rothbury Manor £72 12s 9½d (£72.68); Corbridge Manor £47 6s 8d (£47.34); Newburn Manor £58 11s 1d (£58.56). The balance of the three elements, however, was more even than was the case in Alnwick: demesne £95, tenant rents £91 and manorial appurtenances £71. By comparison, the value of Beanley barony was tiny, amounting to only £12 6s 8d (£12.34) arising from free rents in Beanley, South Middleton and a small piece of demesne land at Wooler.

On the basis of this inadequate evidence, it would seem that Henry, Third Lord Percy had a potential gross income of around £1,200 from his estate. But because the evidence comes almost entirely from the inquests *post mortem*, which tend to underestimate true value, it is likely that the figure was substantially higher. Whatever the true figure, Henry, Third Lord Percy was a wealthy man but, as will become apparent later, his successor, the First Earl of Northumberland, enjoyed a larger rent income as the result of his successful estate expansion policy.

TWO

A World of Opportunity, 1368–89

In the twenty-one years between 1368 and 1389, the leading members of the Percy family experienced very considerable success in their public and private lives. The head of the family, Henry, Fourth Lord Percy, enlarged his estate and was raised to the peerage as the First Earl of Northumberland; his younger brother, Sir Thomas Percy (later to become Earl of Worcester and a leading courtier), had a successful military and diplomatic career; and his eldest son, Sir Henry Percy, became famous as a soldier, earning the sobriquet 'Hotspur', by which he has been known ever since, and married a member of the royal family.

Their success stemmed primarily from their ability to take advantage of the opportunities presented by the circumstances of the time. The most imperative of these was war. In 1369, war, which had been brought to an end in 1360, was restarted. Usually known as the Hundred Years War between England and France, it was in reality of much longer duration and was European in its scope. At its heart, however, was the conflict between England on the one hand and France and Scotland on the other that had begun in the mid-1290s. At issue in both cases was the question of **liege homage**.

In Scotland, following the deaths of Alexander III in 1286 and his granddaughter, Margaret, in 1290, Edward I of England adjudicated the rival claims to the throne of the Balliol and Bruce families, cadet branches of the royal house. His decision in 1292 went in favour of John Balliol, the senior of the two contenders. What provoked the conflict was Edward's insistance that John owed liege homage to him, with all that that entailed. John's resistance, triggered by Edward's demand that he should furnish Scottish troops for a campaign in France, led to an English invasion and to John's deposition and banishment in 1296. However, Edward's attempt to conquer Scotland failed and ten years later, Robert Bruce, grandson of the

The Scottish Royal Family

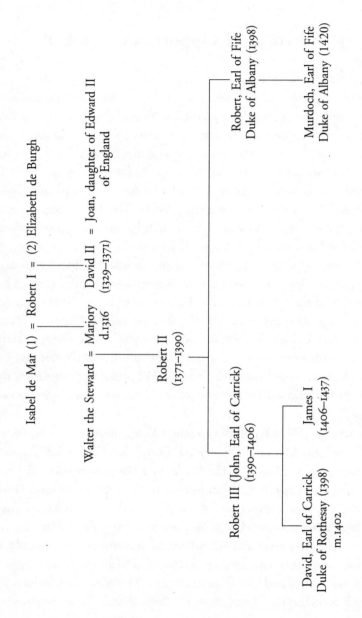

rejected candidate of 1292, had himself crowned King of Scots. It took him twenty-two years of almost constant war to make good his claim. But in 1328, the year before his death, the illicit government of Queen Isabelle and her lover, Roger Mortimer (who had deposed and murdered her husband, Edward II, the previous year) conceded to Bruce his right to be Robert I of Scotland in full sovereignty.

The following year, however, the young Edward III removed his mother and Mortimer from power, rejected her 'shameful peace' and renewed his grandfather's effort to subjugate Scotland by giving his support to the attempt by Edward Balliol, the heir of John Balliol who had died in 1314, to regain his father's throne. We cannot be certain what Edward's ambition towards Scotland was, but it is likely that he was not really interested in conquest so much as having a subservient king holding the kingdom by liege homage. That he did not succeed in this was primarily due to a change in direction of his foreign policy in the late 1330s.

Anglo-French hostility also centred on the question of liege homage, but in reverse: it was the King of England of whom liege homage was demanded by the King of France. The territory at issue was the Duchy of Aquitaine (which was also called Guienne). The legal and constitutional question was compounded by the disputed extent of the duchy. Its irreduceable core, however, was Gascony, bounded by the Atlantic, the Pyrenees and the River Garonne. The duchy was the remnant of Henry II's huge empire that also had included Normandy, Maine, Anjou and Touraine. These provinces had been lost to the English Crown in the early thirteenth century, but in 1259, Henry III of England and his French counterpart, Louis IX, concluded a peace treaty whereby Aquitaine was ceded to England. But on what terms? The French had no doubt that it was to be held by the King of England by liege homage. The English, however, claimed that their king should hold it in full sovereignty. It was the uncompromising approach to this problem by the French king, Philippe IV (1285–1314) that led to war.

To the Aquitaine Question was added Edward III's claim to the French throne, which was well founded. Following Philippe IV's death, the crown passed in rapid succession to his three sons, none of whom had a male heir. When the last, Charles IV, died in 1328, there was no incontrovertible successor. The decision went in favour of Philippe, Count of Valois, cousin of the three deceased kings, who assumed the title of 'Philippe VI'. But this decision ignored the claim of Edward III, whose mother, Isabelle, was Philippe IV's daughter. The infamous Salic Law, which supposedly confined the French throne to males, was in fact of no great antiquity and had been recently confected to meet this situation.

Edward III laid claim to the French throne in 1337 and formally adopted the title 'King of France' in 1340 as a move in the complex diplomacy that followed Philippe VI's confiscation of the Duchy of Aquitaine. As with Scotland, it is not certain that Edward's real ambition was to become King of France. In the end he was prepared to relinquish his claim in return for full sovereignty in Aquitaine. This in fact was the essence of the Treaty of Bretigny, agreed but never fully ratified in 1360.

The second phase of the war was to be of longer duration and wider geographical spread. It was also fought with greater intensity. It has been calculated by J.J.N. Palmer that between 1337 and 1360 there was military action in only eight of the twenty-three years and that the English launched a mere eight major expeditions, but between 1369 and 1389 fighting took place in all but four years and there were fourteen major expeditions that lasted longer and ranged more widely. Also in contrast to the earlier phase, the English enjoyed few spectacular successes and there were occasions in the 1380s when there was a serious prospect of a major French invasion of England. All told, there was little prospect of forcing the issue: stalemate seemed to be a permanent condition.

The underlying reasons for this were threefold. The first was that the French (and also the Scots) deliberately avoided battle. This is understandable in the light of the catastrophic defeats both had suffered, the Scots at Neville's Cross (1346) and the French at Crecy (1346) and Poitiers (1356). Neither the French nor the Scots had yet found the answer to the English battle tactic developed in the 1330s of combining heavily armed and armoured men at arms fighting on foot alongside archers wielding the fearsome longbow with its capacity to kill at up to 200 yards. As well as military disasters, Neville's Cross and Poitiers were also political catastrophes: at the former David II was captured and remained a prisoner until 1357; and at the latter, Jean II became a prisoner and died in captivity in 1364.

The English Royal Family

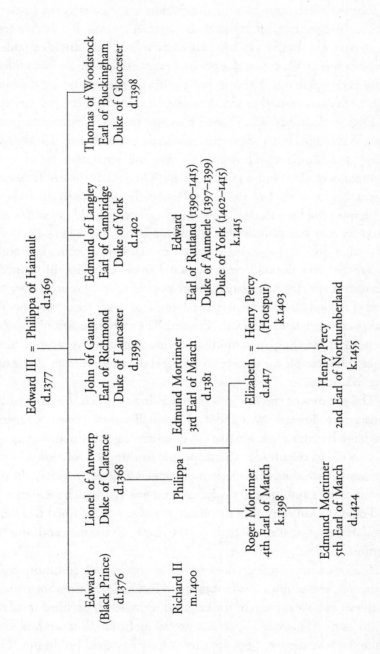

Edward III = Philippa of Hainault
d.1377   d.1369

Edward (Black Prince) d.1376

Richard II m.1400

Lionel of Antwerp Duke of Clarence d.1368

Philippa = Edmund Mortimer 3rd Earl of March d.1381

Roger Mortimer 4th Earl of March k.1398

Edmund Mortimer 5th Earl of March d.1424

Elizabeth = Henry Percy (Hotspur) d.1417   k.1403

Henry Percy 2nd Earl of Northumberland k.1455

John of Gaunt Earl of Richmond Duke of Lancaster d.1399

Edmund of Langley Earl of Cambridge Duke of York d.1402

Edward Earl of Rutland (1390–1415) Duke of Aumerle (1397–1399) Duke of York (1402–1415) k.1415

Thomas of Woodstock Earl of Buckingham Duke of Gloucester d.1398

Earlier defeats bred circumspection, and consequently the French tactic was to counter English invasions by retreat, evasion and harassment. For their part, the English conducted *chevauchées,* long-distance raids across France, which were popular with their participants as (hopefully) they yielded rich pickings. Their strategic purpose was to provoke the French to risk battle, suffer another disastrous defeat and as a consequence capitulate to English demands. The French were not tempted: *chevauchées* may have been damaging, but they were considered preferable to disasters such as Crecy and Poitiers. Allied to this was the emergence of able French commanders, Bertrand du Guesclin and Olivier de Clisson, for whom war was a business to be waged professionally and with clear objectives. Underpinning his successes were the policies of Charles V, who succeeded his father, the quixotically chivalrous Jean II, as king in 1364. He developed a taxation system that enabled France to maintain a permanent army, and it was he who decided that pitched battles were not in France's best interest. As France was a larger, more populous and a much richer country than England, once it had geared itself to war, there was no realistic prospect of England achieving Edward III's grandiose aim of conquest. At the same time, England's military ability and capacity were sufficient to make it impossible for the French to expel the English from all the territory they occupied.

The progress of the war in Scotland followed much the same pattern. In contrast to France, Scotland was a smaller and poorer country than England, but this did not make conquest any easier. Much of its geography was hostile to the invader and its people had devised ways of surviving the occasional invasion. But perhaps its greatest asset was that the English government's ambition towards Scotland was very much secondary to that in France. As in the previous phase, war was not confined to France and Scotland, but spilled over into the Low Countries and the Iberian Peninsula.

The other outstanding characteristic of this period, common to all three countries, was political disharmony and instability arising from inadequate or unsatisfactory monarchs. In England, Edward III declined in all respects in the 1370s. This was in part due to failing health, but the loss of Queen Philippa, who died in 1369, appears to have hastened his decline. His final years were notable for his dependence on his mistress, Alice Perrers, allegations of financial maladministration, and in the end his senility. To make the situation worse, his heir, Edward, the Black Prince, predeceased him by a few months, after a long decline in health due to dysentery contracted in Spain. The consequence was that upon his death at the age of sixty-four on 21 June 1377, he was succeeded by the Black Prince's ten-year-old son, Richard II. The largest figure in public life was the young king's oldest surviving uncle, John of Gaunt, Duke of Lancaster, and he was to remain so in many respects until his death in 1399. Richard took control of government in the 1380s, but his actions and personality were not such as to promote ease and harmony. His most obvious handicap was that, unlike his father and grandfather, he was no warrior, his liking for matters martial not extending beyond presiding at tournaments.

In Scotland, the throne was occupied in succession by two inadequate kings. The first was David II's nephew, Robert II (1371–90), the son of Robert I's daughter, Marjorie, and Walter the Steward. Fifty-five years old at the time of his accession, he eventually came to be considered unfit to exercise power. In 1384, government was effectively transferred to his heir, John, Earl of Carrick. Four years later, however, Carrick, who had been incapacitated by a kick from a horse, was replaced by his brother, Robert, Earl of Fife. Nevertheless, when Robert II died in 1390, John, Earl of Carrick succeeded to the throne, although changing his name to Robert to become Robert III. To have been King John II would have given legitimacy to King John I (1292–96) of the rival Balliol family. Like his father, the new king was in his early fifties at the time of his accession and, also like his father, he too proved to be inadequate. Consequently, political power continued to be wielded by other members of the royal family: Robert, Earl of Fife, who became Duke of Albany in 1398, and for three years between 1399 and 1402, by the king's heir, David, Duke of Rothesay.

Royal power was largely indirect in the southern areas of Scotland, however. The controlling forces there were George Dunbar, Earl of March, who was dominant in Berwickshire and East Lothian, and Archibald (known as the Grim), Third Earl of Douglas, the illegitimate son of Robert I's chief supporter, Sir James Douglas (known as 'Good Sir James'). His power base was in the west, which he expanded so that by

1372 he was master of the ancient province of Galloway (the counties of Dumfries, Kirkcudbright and Wigtown). His territory was extended eastwards considerably in 1388 by his succession to the earldom of Douglas on the death without legitimate heirs of James, Second Earl of Douglas.

France enjoyed effective government under Charles V, who reigned from 1364 until 1380. His successor, Charles VI, was not of the same calibre and, to make matters worse, from 1392 until his death in 1422, he suffered from recurring bouts of insanity. Consequently, the political life of France was for long periods disputed ground between two other members of the royal family: the king's uncle, Philippe (known as the Bold), Duke of Burgundy, and the king's younger brother, Louis, Duke of Orleans. It was the former who was dominant during the periods of royal lucidity, the latter coming to the fore when the king descended into insanity. Philippe's power was increased considerably in 1384 when he became Count of Flanders following the death of his father-in-law, Louis de Maele, Count of Flanders, whose only child, his daughter Margaret, he had married in 1369. This marriage was a major diplomatic coup for Charles V of France in that it thwarted the proposed union of Margaret and Edmund of Langley, Edward III's fourth son.

The war also had a diplomatic aspect, although between 1379 and 1413 the scope for successful international diplomacy was hampered by the Great Schism. During this period there were always two popes following the double election in 1379 of the Italian, Bartolomeo Prignano, as Urban VI and the Frenchman, Robert of Geneva, as Clement VII. Inevitably, the states of Europe took sides. Since England chose to recognise Urban, France and Scotland opted to support Clement. The ability of the papacy to perform its traditional role as a mediator and arbitrator in international disputes was therefore significantly diluted.

This, then, was the world in which the Fourth Lord Percy, who at the age of twenty-six succeeded his father in May 1368, was to live and experience for the following twenty years. He was twenty-six years old. By 1389, he had three major accomplishments to his credit: he had secured the elevation of his family to the ranks of the nobility; he had made advantageous marriages for himself and all his children; and he had substantially augmented the Percy estate. Most of what he acquired he

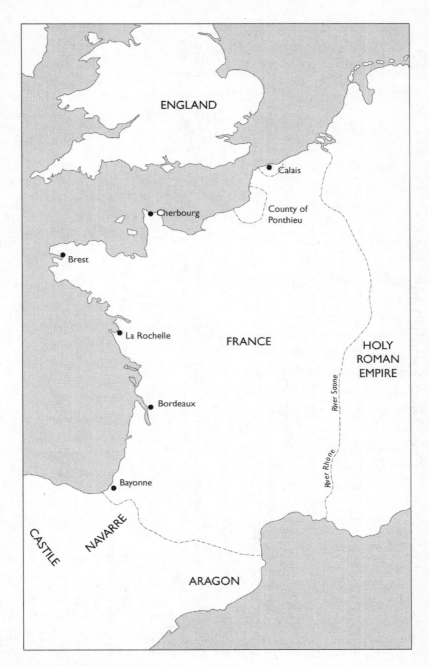

France and her neighbours

The Percy Family 1368–1455

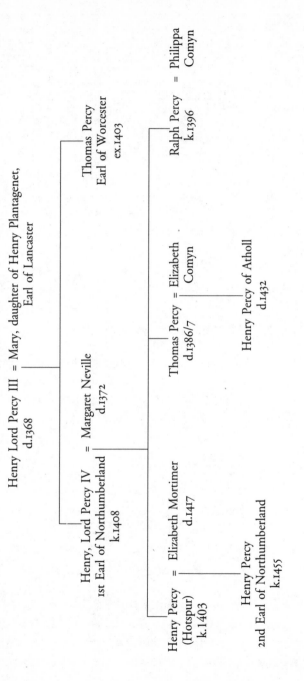

Henry Lord Percy III = Mary, daughter of Henry Plantagenet,
d.1368   Earl of Lancaster

Thomas Percy
Earl of Worcester
ex.1403

= Margaret Neville
   d.1372

Henry, Lord Percy IV
1st Earl of Northumberland
k.1408

Ralph Percy
k.1396

= Philippa
   Comyn

Thomas Percy = Elizabeth
d.1386/7   Comyn

Henry Percy of Atholl
d.1432

Henry Percy = Elizabeth Mortimer
(Hotspur)   d.1447
k.1403

Henry Percy
2nd Earl of Northumberland
k.1455

retained in his own hands, but he used some of his gains to endow his sons, notably his heir, Sir Henry Percy, but also his younger sons, Thomas and Ralph.

In advancing his wealth and status, he had an advantageous start in that his mother, Mary Plantagenet, was the sister of Henry, Earl (and from 1351 Duke) of Lancaster, a grandson of Henry III. He was therefore the king's cousin. Added to this was an upbringing in the glittering and sophisticated household of the Duke of Lancaster. And it was as a member of that household that he began his public career as one of the duke's **retinue** on the great expedition of 1359, which it was hoped would end with the coronation of Edward III as King of France at Rheims. The death of his patron two years later did not hinder his progress. His military activities were sufficiently distinguished for him to be made a Knight of the Garter in 1366, and ten years later to secure him the post of Marshal, joint commander with the Constable, of the king's army.

The following year he joined the ranks of the higher nobility as Earl of Northumberland. The occasion was the coronation of Richard II on 16 July, when he and three other men were given the title 'earl' in what seems to have been a coronation honours list. The earldom was in recognition of his status in Northumberland and the important role he was expected to play in the defence of the northern border at a time when the situation there had again become dangerous and uncertain.

His qualification for comital status was enhanced by two important territorial gains he made in Northumberland and Cumberland in 1381, both from long-established families of Norman origin: the Umfravilles and the Lucys. The Umfravilles had been major landowners in Northumberland since the time of William II and Henry I, from whom they received the barony of Prudhoe and the Liberty of Redesdale. In 1243, they acquired the Scottish earldom of Angus through the marriage of Gilbert de Umfraville and Maud, the daughter and heir of John Comyn, Earl of Angus.

The transfer of Umfraville property to the Percys was effected by Gilbert de Umfraville's great grandson, also Gilbert de Umfraville (born 1325), who, although still styled 'Earl of Angus' in England, had ceased to be so regarded in Scotland. Umfraville was twice married. By his first wife, Joan, daughter of the First Lord Willoughby, he had three sons, all of whom died young. Joan herself died in 1350 and sometime later he married Maud Lucy. This marriage proved barren, and consequently on 16 August 1375, at the age of sixty-five years, he created a settlement whereby the barony of Prudhoe in Northumberland, and also the Lincolnshire manors of Burwell and Calceby, were settled on himself and his wife for life with remainder to the heirs of their bodies and subsequent remainder to Henry Percy. In return, Percy granted him an **annuity** of £40. The same arrangement was made for the Liberty of Redesdale in Northumberland and for the rest of their Lincolnshire properties, except that the subsequent remainder was to his half-brothers, Robert and Thomas de Umfraville. The explanation for this otherwise curious decision may go back to 1340, when Margaret, daughter of the Second Lord Percy (d.1352) was married to Robert, Umfraville's heir by his first wife. Umfraville settled on the couple the barony of Prudhoe, with the proviso that if Robert died in his father's lifetime (which happened) the estate should be held in trust for his widow, with successive reversions to Gilbert and his wife, the heirs of their bodies and then to the Earl and his heirs. It was the death in 1375 of Margaret (who married her second husband, William, Third Lord Ferrers of Groby) that led to the settlement of that year.

To be more certain of securing the property, following Umfraville's death on 6 January 1381, Percy, now First Earl of Northumberland, took the precaution of marrying his widow; and in some haste, since Maud Umfraville is known to have become Maud Percy before the end of the year. He was in a position to do so as he was a widower, his first wife, a daughter of Ralph, Lord Neville and widow of William, Third Lord Ros of Helmsley, whom he married in 1358, having died in 1372.

But there was a more urgent reason for marriage to Maud Umfraville. She was in her own right heir to three important estates: the barony of Langley in Northumberland and in Cumberland the barony of Cockermouth and a third of the barony of Egremont. Maud inherited these in 1369 as the result of the death on 30 September at the age of two of her niece, Joan, the only child of her brother, Anthony, Third Lord Lucy. Cockermouth and Langley were old Lucy properties, but Egremont had come to the family more recently through the marriage of Anthony Lucy's father, Thomas, Second Lord Lucy, and Margaret de Multon, one of the three sisters of the childless John de Multon, who died in 1334.

By his marriage to Maud Umfraville, Percy gained control of these properties, but for life only: on his wife's death, they would pass to her heir in law, Sir William de Melton, the son of Joan, daughter of Anthony, First Lord Lucy, who died in 1343. To ensure that this did not happen and that the estates were retained in his family, he had to persuade his wife to disinherit her distant kinsman. This she agreed to do, entailing her estates on the Earl and herself and the male heir of their bodies, with successive remainders to her husband's eldest son, Sir Henry Percy (Hotspur), his brother, Thomas, and his younger sons, Thomas and Ralph. To this she attached one condition, namely, that the Lucy arms, *gules, three lucies argent* (red ground with three silver pike), should be quartered with those of Percy. The Lucy properties finally became merged into the Percy estate on Maud's death in 1398.

What did these gains amount to? The barony of Prudhoe was of middling size, comprising seven townships in demesne and eight feudal tenancies, all in Northumberland. At its centre was Prudhoe, with its formidable castle on a bluff overlooking the River Tyne and dominating the Newcastle–Carlisle road. With the exception of Kirkwhelpington, the other demesne townships were close at hand in the Tyne Valley at Ovingham, Hedley, Harlow Hill, Horsley and Ingoe. There is no extant valuation for a single year, but scattered evidence suggests an annual value of around £120. The eight feudal tenements, which yielded no income and included ten townships and hamlets, were variously held as one **knight's fee**, four half knight's fees and three fractional fees.

The barony of Langley was the smallest and latest of those created in Northumberland. Its centre at Langley, close to the Tyne Valley and Allendale, was a large tower built in the mid-fourteenth century, possibly by the Third Lord Lucy. Apart from being small in size, it was located in the western part of the county, an upland area of late colonisation. Consequently, its value was not great. In addition to Langley, it comprised eleven demesne settlements: the small borough of Haydon Bridge, the townships of Haydon, Allerwash, Fourstones and Warden and six neighbouring hamlets. The income from these, according to the inquest *post mortem* taken in 1370 following the death of Joan Lucy, was between £30 and £40. There were also fifteen freehold tenements, the most important being Blenkinsop and Featherstone, which brought in just over £5. In all, the barony was worth less than £50 a year.

In Cumberland, the third part of the barony of Egremont comprised five places attached to Egremont (Eskdale, Wasdale Head, Drigg, Ravenglass and Gosforth) and two attached to Loweswater (Thackthwaite and Mockerkin). In 1370, its annual value was just over £30. In contrast, the barony of Cockermouth was large and extensive. It had seven large demesne manors: Cockermouth, Dean, Whinfell, Braithwaite, Papcastle, Aspatria and Wigton, which between them included twenty-seven hamlets. Annual income from these sources, according to the inquest *post mortem*, was little more than £70. To this was added over £12 from twenty-three feudal holdings, comprising payments in lieu of the ancient rent known as **cornage** and of an obligation known as 'watch of the sea'. The total income of little more than £100 must be a very considerable underestimate, since in the early fifteenth century the annual yield of the Percys' Cumberland properties was over £400. But the benefit from the possession of these baronies was more than financial in that it gave the Percys hold over, or influence in, around fifty places in Cumberland and made them a major force in that county. The prospective gain from the Umfraville settlement of 1375 may help to explain the elevation of the Fourth Lord Percy to the earldom of Northumberland two years later, while this newly found status might have influenced Maud Umfraville to marry the Earl and to merge her family's fortunes with his.

The Earl also gained more property in Northumberland from the demise of the Comyn family, who since the twelfth century had held the manor of Tarset covering a huge area in the valley of the North Tyne. As a member of the Liberty of Tynedale, it belonged to the Scottish kings from its creation in the late 1150s until the death of Alexander III in 1286. In 1314, with the deaths of both John Comyn, (the son of the man murdered by Robert Bruce in the Dominican friary in Dumfries in 1306), and of his son, Aimery, the manor was inherited by his two sisters, Joan and Elizabeth. By various means, the Earl contrived to acquire both parts of the manor. Joan Comyn married David, Earl of Atholl, but the male line ended with the death in 1369 of their grandson, also David, leaving as his heirs his two daughters, Elizabeth and Philippa, aged respectively seven and six. The Earl purchased from the Crown the marriage of the two girls, and as soon as they reached the legal age married them to his second and third sons, Thomas to Elizabeth and Ralph to Philippa. This move was only a temporary success. Thomas Percy and Elizabeth had a son, known in adulthood as Sir Thomas Percy of Atholl, who died in 1432. But the marriage of Ralph Percy and Philippa was childless and ended in divorce; consequently, Philippa's property went with her to her second husband.

The younger Comyn heiress, Elizabeth, married twice. Her first husband was a Herefordshire knight, Sir Richard Talbot of Goodrich Castle, by whom she had a son, Gilbert. After Sir Richard's death, she married Sir John Bromwich, who persuaded his step-son to sell his rights in Tarset to him. The probable date was 1379, when Bromwich placed his Tynedale properties and a manor in Herefordshire in trust to his own use. At an unknown date after that, however, he sold the Tynedale estate to the Earl, who must have invested Hotspur with it, since it was among the properties forfeited to the Crown after his death.

The Earl also made gains, some of which did not accrue until after 1389, from the estate of Joan, daughter and sole heir of John, Lord Orreby (Orby in Lincolnshire), who was his father's second wife. By her, his father had a daughter, Mary, the Earl's step-sister, who became the wife of John, Fifth Lord Ros of Helmsley. Mary died childless in August 1394, but in the course of her life she made arrangements for some of her properties to the benefit of her Percy relations. The most conclusive were her grants to the Earl of the manors of Isleham in Cambridgeshire, Cratfield in Suffolk and Toft by Witham and Dalby in Wainfleet in Lincolnshire. In addition, she granted to the Earl and his brother, Thomas Percy, an annual rent of £40 from the manor of Bradwell in Essex. She also assigned rents totalling £50 from three more Essex manors, Dengie, Pilton and Hockley, for the term of his life to William Roudon, Rector of Warsop in Nottinghamshire, with remainder to the Earl and his sons, Thomas and Ralph. In doing so, she saddled the heir to these Essex manors, John de la Mare, a citizen of London, with a considerable financial burden.

The situation was made more complicated by an earlier settlement made by John, Lord Orreby's, father, also John. He granted to his son, John, and his daughter-in-law, Margaret, and the heirs of their bodies, the manors of Dronfield in Derbyshire, Hunmanby in Yorkshire, Candleby and Boston, together with land in East Kirkby, Stickford, and Tattersall in Lincolnshire, with remainder to Sir Adam de Clifton and Robert de Barnack. Both men predeceased Mary, so that when the original inheritance line ended with her death in 1394, the heirs were Constantine Clifton and Ralph, Lord Cromwell, whose wife, Maud, was the daughter of Robert de Barnack's brother, John.

These complex arrangements were in no one's interest. Consequently, by means of a convoluted set of negotiations concluded in 1395, they were disentangled, considerably to the benefit of the Percy family. The Earl gained possession of Isleham, Hunmanby, Toft by Witham, Dalby and Bradwell, while his youngest son, Ralph, acquired Dronfield. Cromwell, the other major figure in the deal, acquired what presumably he desired, namely, the Lincolnshire properties close to his seat at Tattersall.

The Earl also added by purchase or escheat six other manors as well as smaller pieces of land to his estate. One manor was Heyshott, close to his Sussex estate at Petworth, purchased from the executors of a Thomas Chamberlayn, and was worth just under £10 a year. The rest were in Yorkshire: the manors of Healaugh, Walton and Linton, all close to York, Wetherby and Tadcaster; and land in Scorborough. In Northumberland, his acquisitions were the manors of Bilton and Fawdon, both of which were members of the Alnwick barony, and an unidentified property called 'Famvun' close to the Cheviot in the north-west of the county.

He also extended his control over the Alnwick barony by means of exchange, persuading the Hilton family to restore to him the lordship of Shilbottle in Northumberland in return for the Yorkshire manors of Bolton Percy, Wharram Percy and Carnaby. The lordship of Shilbottle had been created by the First Lord of Alnwick, Gilbert Tison, for his younger son, Richard, but had passed to the Hiltons with the marriage of Richard's granddaughter and heir, Bona, to William de Hilton c.1200. The lordship comprised Shilbottle, Newton on the Moor, Hazon, Guyzance, and Rennington with its hamlet, Broxfield, and therefore looks more substantial than the three manors granted in exchange. If so, then the Earl

34

may have been guilty of bullying a weaker man. But it is possible that the two estates were approximately equal in value. What seems clear is that the Earl was at pains to consolidate his control of the barony of Alnwick, even if that meant sacrificing properties in Yorkshire.

How much was the Earl worth? Again, the absence of detailed estate managers' accounts makes accurate calculations impossible. Perhaps the most useful guide is the assessment of J.W.M. Bean, who reckoned that the Earl's grandson at the time of his death in 1455 had a potential gross income of £2,825, all but £325 coming from the estates in Northumberland, Cumberland and Yorkshire. Although the estate in 1455 was not quite as large as it had been in 1400, the difference was marginal, not substantial. And by way of balance, it is almost certain that between 1400 and 1450 the economic situation in the North East became more fragile, so that rents may have been lower in the latter year. If £2,825 or something close to it is a correct estimate of income for the last years of the Earl's life, it reinforces the view that the income he inherited was considerably greater than the £1,200 suggested by the inquests *post mortem*: the Earl had undoubtedly increased the size of the estate, but not by so much as to more than double its yield.

It is important to remember, however, that the Earl's income did not derive exclusively from land. For much of his career he was one of the wardens of the marches, offices that carried substantial fees. That of the East March, with which normally went the post of Keeper of Berwick, was the more important and carried a higher remuneration: £3,000 in time of peace but £12,000 in time of war. The Warden of the West March, who was also Keeper of Carlisle, had smaller fees of £1,500 in peace and £6,000 in war. For the Earl, therefore, that he or his son should be Warden of the East March was of significant financial importance; and for both wardenships to be in Percy hands was even better. Also possible was a further £4,000 for keeping the strategically important Scottish castle of Roxburgh, which remained in English hands until 1460. However, unlike land rents, these public offices were in the gift of the Crown. This meant uncertainty of appointment and tenure and uncertainty of payment. The policy of the Crown was not to allow the Percys or anyone else to monopolise the wardenships and keeperships; and it also had the power to fob off the wardens with less than their dues: J.W.M. Bean has calculated that the Earl's grandson received only 69 per cent of the money due to him.

About the Earl's brother, Sir Thomas Percy, there is much less information. Even his exact date of birth is not known, although it was probably in 1343. And there is no evidence that he ever married or had children. His finances are also shadowy. In 1368, his father entailed on him the manors of Wressle (where he built a castle) and two other places in the East Riding of Yorkshire, Claxby in Lincolnshire and Foston in Leicestershire, which would have given him a basic income. To this, his sister-in-law, Maud Umfraville, added the reversion of the manor of Radstone, an outcome not achieved until the death in 1400 of its holder, Edward III's former mistress, Alice Perrers, and, as noted above, he had an annuity from the Essex manor of Bradwell. He may also have drawn income from the manors of Amersham, Buckland and Singleborough in Buckinghamshire, granted to him and Hugh Despenser by Thomas, Lord Despenser. The arrangement bears the hallmarks of an **enfeoffment to use**, but it was said that they, that is Thomas and Hugh, 'took the profits and still do'. In addition, like others close to the centre of power, Thomas was able to profit through grants of the wardship and marriage of minors, as for example the heir of the Yorkshire knight, Sir Brian Stapleton. This was originally granted to William Lescrope, Earl of Wiltshire, who, for unstated reasons, then released the wardship to Thomas Percy. Thomas, however, chose not to exploit this asset directly, but leased it to Sir Robert Hilton for an annual rent of £20. In doing so, he deprived himself of a further £40 income. In addition, after 1374 he had an annual pension of £100, awarded to him by Edward III as a reward for his services in Poitou. Clearly he was not a poor man but, as we shall see, it was in the last ten years of Richard II's reign that Thomas Percy became wealthy, but largely as the result of fees arising from state service, not land rents.

The third important Percy was the Earl's eldest son and heir-apparent, Sir Henry Percy, known as 'Hotspur', a sobriquet given to him by the Scots. Born on 20 May 1364, he is known to have been physically precocious, being first in arms as early as 1378 at the siege of Berwick, when he was only fourteen. He did not reach his majority until 1385, and therefore it was not until the 1390s that he made major gains in Northumberland. He did so through the efforts made by the Earl to benefit from the consequences of the murder in December 1363 of John de Coupland. This man came to prominence in 1346 as the captor of David II of Scotland as he fled the battle of Neville's Cross. His material reward was considerable, and he used it, together with his frequent tenure of the office of Sheriff of Northumberland, to accumulate a considerable estate in that county, particularly in the baronies of Wark on Tweed and Wooler. It was his aggressive empire-building that led to his murder at the instigation of members of the north Northumberland gentry.

The barony of Wark on Tweed was in the hands of three generations of the Montague family from 1329 until 1397, but Coupland leased it from them sometime in the 1350s, an arrangement continued by his widow after his death. In addition, he acquired four manors within the barony: Mindrum, Presson, Kilham and Paston. His gains in Wooler Barony were greater. This barony was divided into three upon the death of Robert de Muschamp III in 1250, the parts passing to the husbands of his three daughters. Within five years, however, the number of parts was reduced to two as the result of the death of one of the women. Subsequently, the two halves passed to the descendants or successors of Isabel Muschamp and her husband, William de Huntercombe, and Marjory Muschamp and her husband, Malise Graham, Earl of Strathern. It was the Huntercombe portion that Coupland acquired in 1351 from Sir John Lilburn. This gave him the lordship of no fewer than twelve manors: Antechester and Trollop in the Cheviot Forest, Coupland, Yeavering, Akeld, Ford, Crookham, Kimmerston, a quarter of Hethpool, Outchester, Detchant, Barmoor and the farm known as Unthank. He made two further gains: one was the manor of Newham in the barony of Alnwick; the other was the manor of Byker on the western edge of Newcastle upon Tyne. The rent of 200 marks (£133.34) agreed by Joan de Coupland in 1365 when renewing the lease of the Wark properties, gives some idea of the wealth accumulated by her husband and helps to explain the local animosity towards him that almost certainly accounts for his murder.

On his death, all of these properties passed to his widow, Joan, a member of another north Northumberland family of long standing, the Strothers of Kirknewton. And to this substantial portfolio she added two manors in Ellingham Barony – Ellingham and Newstead (which included the now non-existent settlement of Osberwyk) – and a further one – Warenford – in Wooler Barony. These manors had belonged to, respectively, John de Clifford and Henry de Lucker, the men deemed responsible for her husband's murder, who were required to hand over their property to her as compensation.

Joan de Coupland retained all her inherited and acquired estates until 1372, when she sold out to Sir Richard Fitzalan, who became Earl of Arundel and Surrey in 1376 and was executed in 1397. Thereafter, the story lacks certainty. There is evidence that not long after 1372 Arundel turned over the accumulation to his brother, Sir John Arundel. He was killed in 1379, but two years earlier he had placed it in the hands of a trust headed by their brother, Thomas Arundel, Bishop of Ely. However, there is contrary evidence that Sir Richard Fitzalan enfeoffed eight men, including the Earl, Sir Thomas Percy and Hotspur, with all but four of the properties, and that they subsequently released their rights to Hotspur. The properties not included, that is, Byker, Ellingham, Newham and Newstead, were subject to a mortgage to Hotspur in the sum of 500 marks (£333.34). The only way to reconcile the two versions is to believe that Sir John Arundel's trustees sold out to Hotspur, probably in the mid-1390s. What is clear, however, is that when Hotspur's son was restored in 1416, he succeeded in recovering only the four places mortgaged to his father, the mortgage it must be assumed having not been redeemed. The other lands were restored to the Arundels in 1400 in the person of a Sir Richard Arundel. He was described as king's knight and also on one occasion as the king's kinsman, but otherwise his identity remains unclear. In 1408, when the Earl, Thomas Percy and Hotspur were dead, Arundel sold the property to Sir Thomas Grey of Heaton (whose father had acquired the Barony of Wark in 1398) and who came of age the previous year. In 1415, he was executed at Southampton for his part in the conspiracy to murder Henry V as he prepared to embark for France.

Hotspur also possessed very briefly small amounts of land at Bishopton, Little Stainton, Newbiggin, Barmpton and Hedley in the Palatinate of Durham. But after Hotspur's death, a certain John Gilett claimed that the lands were rightfully his and that he had been ejected from them by four men with Hotspur's backing. They then promptly enfeoffed Hotspur with the properties. If this account is true, then Hotspur was prepared to use strong-arm tactics for personal gain. However, another version relates that in 1403 the Gilett family was in possession of the land in Bishopton (which amounted to 89 acres) and had agreed to sell to Hotspur, although again it may have been a sale under duress. The truth of this incident is beyond recovery. What is clear is that as a result of Hotspur's death in the summer of that year the lands were lost to the Percys. Quite why Hotspur should have been bothered with tiny properties in an area where neither he nor his family had any interest is also obscure, unless his long-term aim was to create a strategic Percy presence in the Durham Palatinate.

Of equal if not greater importance than his territorial acquisitions, was Hotspur's marriage, which probably took place in 1379. His wife was Elizabeth (not Catherine as Shakespeare has it), the daughter of Edmund Mortimer, Third Earl of March, the great-grandson of Roger Mortimer, Edward II's queen's lover and co-conspirator. The family recovered its reputation and its huge estates through loyal service to Edward III, so much so that the Third Earl of March was allowed to marry Philippa, the only child of Lionel of Antwerp, Duke of Clarence. He was the second son of Edward III, and his wife, Elizabeth de Burgh, was heir to the earldom of Ulster. Elizabeth Mortimer was therefore at the time of her marriage a granddaughter of the late king and a cousin of the current monarch. By this union, Hotspur had significantly reinforced his family's links with the royal family and any son he had by Elizabeth would have some claim to the throne.

The use to which the Earl put his younger sons, Thomas and Ralph, in the interest of estate aggrandisement has been noted. What befell them may conveniently be dealt with here. Their dates of birth are unknown, but it is likely that they were in the mid to late 1360s. In 1376 or 1377, they were married to the two Comyn sisters, Elizabeth and Philippa, the daughters and joint heirs of David of Stathbogie, who had extensive properties in England, where his Scottish title, Earl of Atholl, continued to be acknowledged, even though in Scotland his family had been stripped of both it and their lands.

Neither man lived long. Thomas Percy died in Castile, probably of disease, in either 1386 or 1387, when he was with his uncle, Sir Thomas Percy, in the service of John of Gaunt. By 1391, his widow, Elizabeth, had remarried, to Sir John Lescrope, a younger son of Lord Scrope of Masham. Thomas and Elizabeth, however, did have a son, Henry, known on account of his maternal ancestry as Sir Henry Percy of Atholl. He died in 1432.

Ralph Percy's life was slightly longer and more interesting and intriguing. In 1384, a judicial investigation was held in Yorkshire into the alleged rape and abduction from the Percy manor of Seamer, near Scarborough, of Ralph's wife, nineteen-year-old Philippa. The accused was a John Halsham, whose name suggests a connection with Halsham, near Hull, in the East Riding. How complicit Philippa was in this affair is not certain, but it seems likely that she was, since by 1391 her marriage to Ralph Percy had been annulled and she had become the wife of the alleged rapist. In fact, the marriage probably took place as early as 1388, for at the time of his death in 1415, Halsham's heir was said to be twenty-four years old, that is, to have been born in 1389. John Halsham later acquired the manor of West Grinstead, where he and Philippa are buried in the parish church of St George.

Like his brother, Ralph Percy too died overseas. He left England in 1396 in order to take part in the crusade that came to grief at Nicopolis, in modern Bulgaria. Why he did so is unclear. As late as December 1395, he was still involved in Border defence as Captain of Berwick, although with a truce in operation, it is possible that he was not in residence. His renown as a warrior was as high as Hotspur's, and therefore, like so many of his contemporaries, he may have found the temptation to enhance his reputation by feats of arms on the frontier of Christendom impossible to resist. To this end, he joined the multinational force organised by the Holy Roman Emperor, Sigismund, the purpose of which was to stem the westward advance of the Ottoman Turks and to save Byzantium (Istanbul). Indiscipline and an unco-ordinated command structure led to a catastrophic defeat at Nicopolis (now Nikopol in Bulgaria) on 25 September 1396 at the hands of the Turkish sultan, Bajazet. Since an inquisition taken at Chesterfield in Derbyshire in January 1400 records his death as having occurred on 15 September 1397, it is possible that he did not die in battle but was killed later as a captive.

John of Gaunt's Family

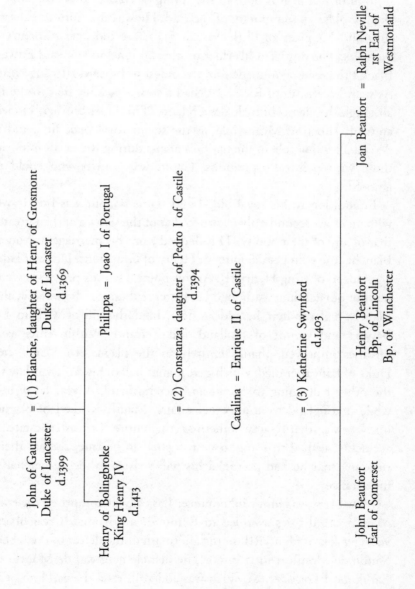

John of Gaunt
Duke of Lancaster
d.1399

= (1) Blanche, daughter of Henry of Grosmont
Duke of Lancaster
d.1369

Henry of Bolingbroke
King Henry IV
d.1413

Philippa = Joao I of Portugal

= (2) Constanza, daughter of Pedro I of Castile
d.1394

Catalina = Enrique II of Castile

= (3) Katherine Swynford
d.1403

John Beaufort
Earl of Somerset

Henry Beaufort
Bp. of Lincoln
Bp. of Winchester

Joan Beaufort = Ralph Neville
1st Earl of
Westmorland

Throughout these years, Percy fortunes became increasingly involved with those of two men: the Earl's cousin, John of Gaunt, Duke of Lancaster and Gaunt's eldest son, Henry of Bolingbroke.

John of Gaunt was born in the spring of 1340 and was therefore a very slightly older contemporary of the Earl. He was the third of Edward III's sons and his place of birth was, as his name indicates, Ghent/Gant in Flanders. The deaths of his elder brothers, Lionel in 1368 and Edward, the Black Prince, in 1376, made him the oldest of Edward III's surviving sons. As such he was, until Richard II had a son, a possible heir to the throne, although the claims of male descendants of his older brother, Lionel, were arguably superior. Meanwhile, as the senior royal male he could not be denied a leading role in the nation's affairs during Richard's minority. For those with political aspirations, Gaunt was a man who could not be ignored.

In addition to his royal blood and status, Gaunt was hugely wealthy, with an estate second only in size to that of the Crown and far greater than that of any of the nobility. This derived from his marriage in May 1359 to Blanche, the younger daughter of Henry of Grosmont, Duke of Lancaster, a grandson of King Henry III. At this point, Gaunt's prospects were good but not outstanding. Although Lancaster had no son, he was still alive and Blanche had a co-heir, her older sister, Maud, the wife of William, Duke of Bavaria and Count of Holland and Zeeland. Within three years his fortunes improved, thanks entirely to the plague. In March 1361, the Duke of Lancaster died, which gave Gaunt half of his father-in-law's estate, the other half going to Maud and her husband. A year later, however, while in England to arrange her affairs, Maud too died of plague. The upshot was that Gaunt inherited the entire Lancaster estate. These accidents seemed to some to be too good to be true, so that there were rumours that he had poisoned his wife's sister to secure her half of the inheritance.

How big was Gaunt's inheritance? Basically, it comprised the collection of estates and titles awarded to Edmund, nicknamed 'Crouchback', the younger son of Henry III, in the aftermath of the defeat of the rebellion of Simon de Montfort in 1265–66. The first element was de Montfort's own Earldom of Leicester, to which was added in 1266 the earldom of Derby, forfeited by another rebel, Robert de Ferrers, and in 1267 the earldom of Lancaster and the lordship of Monmouth. Upon 'Crouchback's' death in 1296, his elder son Thomas inherited all these properties and titles. Thomas increased his wealth by his marriage to the heiress, Alice de Lacy, who between 1306 and 1310 inherited the earldoms of Lincoln and Salisbury, respectively from her father and mother. But in 1322 this vast accumulation of land and titles was forfeit to the Crown as the result of Thomas's failed rebellion against Edward II. However, his brother, Henry, was allowed to succeed to everything, except for the earldom of Salisbury. Henry was blind and died in 1345. His successor was his son, also Henry, known from the place of his birth as Henry of Grosmont. Grosmont was made Earl of Derby in 1337, Earl of Leicester and Earl of Lancaster on the death of his father in 1345 and Earl of Lincoln in 1349 on the death of his grandmother, Alice de Lacy. Two years later, in 1351, he was created Duke of Lancaster.

The estate was scattered over many counties of England and Wales, but its major concentrations were in Lancashire and Yorkshire, the North Midlands and South Wales. A good indication of these concentrations is gained from the list of Gaunt's castles: Lancaster, Liverpool, Clitheroe and Halton (Lancashire), Pontefract, Knaresborough, Pickering and Tickhill (Yorkshire), Tutbury (Staffordshire), Kenilworth (Warwickshire), Leicester and Donnington (Leicestershire), Lincoln and Bolingbroke (Lincolnshire), Kidwelly, Ogmore, Monmouth, Skenfrith, Whitecastle and Grosmont (South Wales), Pleshey (Essex) and Pevensey (Sussex). From this vast agglomeration of properties Gaunt could expect an annual gross income of around £12,000.

The inheritance also included a small outlying element of particular interest to the Percys, namely, the small barony of Embleton on the north Northumberland coast. There, between the Battle of Bannockburn in 1314 and his death in 1322, Earl Thomas of Lancaster built a splendid castle at Dunstanburgh, to which Gaunt was to make improvements in the early 1380s. This constituted a glaring and unwelcome intrusion into what was fast becoming Percy territory.

Blanche of Lancaster did not live long, dying of plague in 1369. Gaunt was thus free to marry again, which he did in 1371. His second wife was of even higher status: Constanza, the elder daughter and designated heir of Pedro I of Castile, who had been deposed and murdered by his half-brother in 1369. At the time the gains from his marriage were no more than honorary and, in material terms, potential. But, given the kaleidoscopic nature of European politics, it was possible that Gaunt might sometime be in a position to make good his claim to be King of Castile and Leon in the right of his wife. And even if this did not come to pass, it added to his bargaining power in the world of international diplomacy. Meanwhile, he was able to style himself 'King of Castile and Leon', in addition to his English dukedom and earldoms.

Ultimately of greater influence on Percy fortunes than John of Gaunt was his heir, Henry, known like other members of the royal family by the place of his birth, the castle of Bolingbroke in Lincolnshire. Born on 30 May 1366, he was almost exactly two years younger than Hotspur. And like Hotspur, he developed into a formidable warrior, earning a considerable reputation as a jouster. In 1385, at the age of nineteen, he was summoned to Parliament as Earl of Derby, one of his father's titles. In 1397, he was to become Duke of Hereford, a title derived from his first wife, Mary, daughter of Humphrey de Bohun, Earl of Hereford, who died in 1373. De Bohun had three comital titles, Hereford, Northampton and Essex, and in addition he was hereditary Constable of England. By his marriage, which took place in 1380 or 1381, Bolingbroke acquired the earldoms of Hereford and Northampton. The Earldom of Essex and the Constableship went to Thomas of Woodstock, Edward III's youngest son, who married Mary's elder sister, Eleanor.

THREE

The Percys in War and Politics, 1368–89

The Percys were, without doubt, a martial family. At any time during the twenty years of war between 1369 and 1389, one or more of them was on campaign in at least one of the many theatres of war. Not all were equally involved, however. The most heavily engaged was Sir Thomas Percy, although Hotspur came a close second. He, however, was still coming to maturity in the early years of this period and therefore did not become prominent until the later 1380s. In contrast, the head of the family played a much less active part in the wars, particularly after he became Earl in 1377. This may have been due to his involvement in national politics and regional administration, of which there is considerable evidence, and also in property acquisition and estate management. Before looking at the military careers of the three men, two points about the war need to be made. The first is that it was broken into two phases by a truce, known as the Truce of Bruges, negotiated by Pope Gregory XI in 1375, which lasted for two years. Secondly, fighting took place in no fewer than seven areas: the Anglo-Scottish border region, Brittany, Aquitaine, other parts of France, Castile and Portugal, the Netherlands and at sea; and in all of these the Percys were involved.

Sir Thomas Percy's involvement is hardly surprising, given that he was the younger brother, unmarried, and with his own fortune to seek. His commitment to war as the means to this end appears to have been wholehearted, and it is clear that he possessed military ability. Moreover, he was equally able in the conduct of diplomacy, the important con-comitant of military activity.

In June 1369, Edward III resumed the title 'King of France' and in November, Charles V of France confiscated Aquitaine from Edward III's heir, Edward, the Black Prince, to whom it had been given in 1362 by his father. By these acts the war with England, which had been ended by the

Treaty of Bretigny in 1360, was restarted. At that time Thomas Percy, who was then probably twenty-five or twenty-six years old, was serving in Aquitaine as Seneschal of La Rochelle, one of the key ports and strong-holds on the Atlantic coast. Given his age and the importance of the post, it is unlikely that he was a new arrival. He may have been in Aquitaine since 1362; and if this was the case, it is probable that he was involved in the Spanish campaign in which the Black Prince had won a notable victory at Najera in April 1367. If so, in whose retinue he served is unknown, but it may have been that of John of Gaunt.

For the Black Prince the Spanish campaign was a military, but not a political, triumph. The years that followed brought disaster: by the end of 1372 French forces directed by Bertrand du Guesclin and Olivier de Clisson had liberated most of Saintonge (between the Gironde and the Charente) and Poitou (between the Charente and the Loire) from English control. In military terms, Thomas Percy was under John Chandos, the

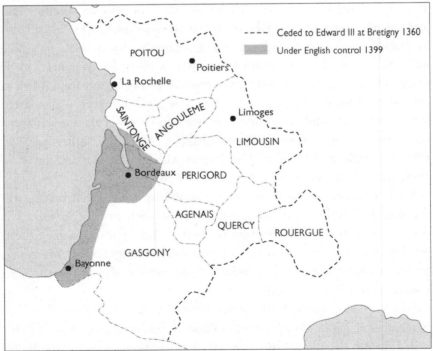

English Gascony

Seneschal of Poitou, a long-time companion of the Black Prince and one of the outstanding soldiers in the first phase of the war.

The situation began to deteriorate at the end of 1370. Late in December, the town of St Savin, twenty-five miles due east of Poitiers, was betrayed to the French. On the 30th, Chandos, accompanied by Percy, made an unsuccessful night attack to recapture it. On the following day, in a skirmish at the bridge over the River Vienne at Lussac, twelve miles to the south-east of St Savin, Chandos was killed, a major loss to English fighting capabilities. It is a testimony to Percy's experience and performance that a few months later he was appointed as Chandos' successor as Seneschal of Poitou.

Almost certainly he was involved in most of the military action in the following months. He was present on 19 September 1370, when, on the orders of the Black Prince, the city of Limoges was sacked: 300 of its inhabitants were massacred and it was rased to the ground, except for its cathedral. The prince's decision was in response to the Bishop of Limoges' desertion to the French camp, an indication that Poitevin loyalties were beginning to waver as those in power began to perceive that the French cause was in the ascendant. Although this incident is appalling to modern beliefs, it was within the rules of war then accepted by all sides. Nevertheless, the prince's reaction was extreme and may have been in part due to his declining health. By this date, he was so debilitated by the amoebic dysentery he had contracted in Spain that a few weeks later he was forced to relinquish his command: on 11 October 1370, he handed over his commission to his brother, John of Gaunt, and in the following March he returned to England. Although Gaunt lacked his elder brother's ability as a soldier, it is hard to see how even a fully fit Black Prince could have permanently stemmed the tide of French advance.

There was, however, one short-lived success for Thomas Percy. In August 1371, he laid siege to Montcontour, a fortress twenty-five miles south of Saumur on the Loire and one of only a handful in Poitou under French control. A French force under de Clisson was sent to prevent this, but Percy secured its surrender before the relieving army arrived. It was to be in English hands for less than a year.

The reason for this was the disasters that befell both Thomas Percy and the plans of the English government in the second half of 1372. The train of events began on 23 June, when a fleet from England under the command of John Hastings, Earl of Pembroke, was totally destroyed off La Rochelle by a fleet of Castilian galleys. Hastings' mission was to bring funds amounting to £12,000 wherewith to raise a local army to resist the French advance. The loss of this money aborted the campaign and in the course of the following months, the westward French advance was largely unchecked.

It is a testimony to the rapidity of the collapse of English control that by the late summer of 1372 the war was being fought on the Atlantic coast of Saintonge, not near the northern and eastern boundaries of Poitou. The fortress of Soubise guarding the mouth of the Charente was under siege by a French force. Thomas Percy and Jean de Grailly, the Captal de Buch, one of the leading Gascon commanders loyal to the English cause, managed to surprise the besiegers and drove them off, taking many prisoners. But immediately the tables were turned: in the middle of the night the English camp was attacked by a French force led by a Welshman, Owain ap Thomas. Both Percy and de Grailly were taken prisoner and, a few days later, La Rochelle capitulated to the French. Percy remained in captivity until he was ransomed on 2 October 1374. Although he had failed as Seneschal of Poitou, it seems that Percy was not disgraced: to secure his release, the English government was prepared to surrender a castle, and on his return to England Edward III awarded him an annual pension for life of £100.

Captivity and the Truce of Bruges, together with affairs in England, meant that Percy was mostly out of armour until 1378, although he became Constable of Roxburgh Castle in 1376 and was involved in measures to keep the truce along the Border. He then became heavily involved in the war in Brittany, where in 1377 England secured from Duke Jean IV the lease of the port and fortress of Brest to be one of its 'barbicans' along the French coast. The strategic thinking was that a line of coastal fortresses would serve defensively to give control of the Channel and prevent raids on the south coast of England, and offensively to act as jumping-off points for *chevauchées*. In pursuit of this concept, Cherbourg was leased about the same time from Charles 'the Bad', King of Navarre, who needed English support in defending his Pyrenean kingdom from Enrique II of Castile. In the following years, the same policy led to unsuccessful attempts to capture St Malo, Harfleur and Nantes.

Thomas Percy was heavily involved in the Breton part of this strategy in association with Thomas of Woodstock, Earl of Buckingham, Edward III's youngest son, who was to become Duke of Gloucester in 1385. It was with Buckingham that he gained naval experience. In 1378, he was made Admiral of the North, commanding the naval forces between the Thames and the Scottish border. In this capacity he had a notable success in December, capturing twenty-two out of a fleet of forty Flemish and Castilian merchant ships, and in the following year he and his fellow admiral, Sir Hugh Calverley, had further success in the Channel and escorted the Duke of Brittany, Jean IV, back to his duchy.

In the same year, he and Calverley were appointed joint Captains of Brest, to command the garrison of the fortress. In September 1381, he became sole commander and continued in that role until January 1386. As many of his duties could be discharged by a deputy, he was not required to be in permanent residence. This enabled him to be part of the Earl of Buckingham's major *chevauchée*, which was launched from Calais in July 1380. It lasted until October and it ranged as far south and east as Rheims and Troyes before turning west to end in Brittany. Buckingham's force was made up of thirteen retinues, of which Thomas Percy's was one of the largest, comprising six knights, 193 **esquires** and 200 archers. Following this raid, Percy took part in Buckingham's abortive attempt to capture Nantes that lasted from November 1380 until the following January. In that month, however, England's Breton policy was undermined when Duke Jean decided to change sides: on 15 January he renounced his alliance with England and did homage for his duchy to the new French king, Charles VI. Although the duchy was now enemy territory, Brest remained in English hands until the late 1390s.

During the next five years Thomas Percy was involved in political matters in England. But in 1386, he relinquished his command at Brest in order to join up with John of Gaunt who was assembling an army with the aim of making good his claim to the throne of Castile. The circumstances that led to this expedition began in 1383, with Fernando I of Portugal. His only legitimate child, his daughter, Beatriz, was married to Juan I of Castile, the son of Enrique II, who succeeded his father in 1379. As a condition of marriage, Juan had promised not to attempt to become king of Portugal, but in 1385 he reneged. To maintain their independence, the Portuguese turned to Fernando's half-brother, Joao, who had the double disability of being illegitimate and, as the head of the Knights of Avis, in monastic orders. He put his military training to good use, inflicting a crushing defeat on the invading Castilian army at Aljubarrota in August 1385. By popular acclaim, he became King Joao I of Portugal. Percy's motives in joining Gaunt's venture may not have been solely military. As will be discussed later, by 1386 the political situation in England was turning ugly as a group of nobles, headed by Thomas of Woodstock, now Duke of Gloucester, began seriously to oppose the youthful Richard II and to campaign against his closest advisers. Percy may have preferred to be out of the way in Castile, risking military rather than political danger.

Gaunt got government approval for his expedition, but very little financial backing. Despite this, he managed to raise an army of 2,000 men at arms and 3,000 archers. Thomas Percy was among those who

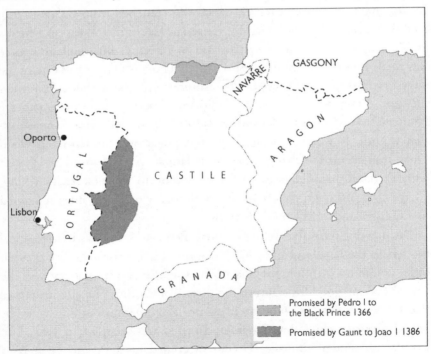

Iberian Peninsula

supplied a retinue, in his case 80 men at arms and 160 archers, for a period of six months. It was a sign of Gaunt's difficulties arising from inadequate funding that he agreed to Percy retaining all the profits of war made by him and his men, except from politically important prisoners. Percy was also Admiral of the Fleet and as such was one of the three senior commanders, the others being the Constable, Sir John Holand (Richard II's half-brother), and the Marshal, Sir Richard Burley.

Percy discharged the first of his duties successfully, bringing the fleet safely from Plymouth to La Coruna. The voyage lasted from 9 to 25 July. During the summer and autumn of 1386, Gaunt was able to consolidate his hold over the province of Galicia, including the important pilgrimage centre of Santiago de Compostella. His success was due less to military victory than to Juan I's decision to trade space for time, knowing that winter and disease might well do his work for him. And so it proved. The major consequence was that Gaunt needed an ally and this led to the agreement made at Ponte do Mouro during the first days of November between Gaunt and Joao I. Almost certainly Percy was one of the negotiators of this alliance, the most important parts of which were that Joao should marry Philippa, Gaunt's daughter by his first wife, Blanche of Lancaster, and in the spring of the following year that he would join with Gaunt in an invasion of Castile. This, it was hoped, would end with the defeat of Juan and the accession coronation of Gaunt to the throne of Castile. The price Gaunt was willing to pay was the cession of a strip of Castilian land along the frontier with Portugal. Percy, together with the Constable and the Marshal, ceremonially escorted Philippa to Oporto for her marriage on 2 February 1387.

Percy then returned to take part in the Anglo-Portuguese invasion of Castile between March and June 1387. By that time the English contingent had been reduced by disease to no more than 1,500 men. Among the deaths was that of Percy's nephew, Thomas Percy, the Earl of Northumberland's second son, who was then about twenty and probably on his first major campaign. The invasion was a fiasco: the allies were not in harmony and the Castilians continued to refuse battle, a tactic urged on them by their French advisers. The military solution having failed, diplomacy was the only option. Fortunately for Gaunt, Juan of Castile was ready to talk: his treasury was empty and he believed the false rumours circulated by Gaunt that reinforcements were on their way from England.

Gaunt appointed Percy to lead the English negotiating team that met their Castilian counterparts at Trancoso. The discussions were protracted, but out of them came a definitive treaty, which was eventually sealed at Bayonne in Gascony on 8 July 1388, with Percy as one of its main witnesses. By its terms, Gaunt agreed to renounce his claim to the Castilian throne. In return, Juan married Catalina (Catherine), Gaunt's daughter by his second, Castilian, wife, Constanza, and agreed to pay Gaunt a lump sum of 600,000 francs and an annual pension of 40,000 francs. It was perhaps because he had been the chief negotiator that Percy was sent to England in late 1387 or early 1388 to brief the government on these developments and, because the agreement had serious diplomatic ramifications, to secure its approval. This was granted, largely because at that moment England was in the throes of a political crisis.

Returning to Gascony, Percy brought reinforcements to Gaunt, but to replace the losses sustained in Castile, not to launch a fresh invasion. Although the government had approved the settlement Percy had negotiated, it was aware that it had done nothing to break the Franco-Castilian alliance: Gaunt may have benefited from it, but England had not. Consequently, in the hope of ending this alliance, Gaunt sent a negotiating team, which included Percy, to hold talks with King Juan of Castile in 1389. But to no avail: although Juan wished for peace, he was not prepared to end his French connection, except as part of a general European settlement.

In the first years after he succeeded his father, the Earl (at that time Henry, Fourth Lord Percy) was as involved in war as his brother. He took part in the *chevauchée* that Gaunt conducted in 1369, which began at Calais and ended at Harfleur, having devastated the Pays de Caux. Percy was a **banneret** commanding a large retinue of 12 knights, 47 esquires and 100 archers. Two years later, he took part in the expedition that attempted to retrieve Pembroke's disaster at La Rochelle. The following year, he joined the most spectacular of the *chevauchées* of these years that led by Gaunt from Calais to Bordeaux between August and October 1373. Percy was again a banneret, but with a much larger retinue comprising 24 knights, 175 esquires and 300 archers.

Thereafter, and particularly after he became Earl of Northumberland, Henry Percy ceased to be concerned with the war in France. Instead, his involvement was with the conflict with Scotland. This flowed along lines very similar to that against France. Like the French, the problem faced by the Scots was liberating those parts of their country that had been under English control since the 1340s and 1350s. As in France, the English government had established 'barbicans' in Scotland at Berwick, Roxburgh, Jedburgh and Lochmaben. But there was an important difference between the two theatres of war. In France, England was active and aggressive in pursuit of the aim of forcing the French to concede full sovereignty over Aquitaine. In Scotland, England's ambition was essentially passive: to hold what she already held. Consequently, in 1370 England negotiated a fourteen-year truce that was to last until Candlemas (2 February) 1384.

For the Scots, however, England's preoccupation with France was their opportunity to regain their lost territories. By the time of the Treaty of Bruges, George Dunbar, Earl of March, had regained control of Berwickshire, except for Berwick and its immediate neighbourhood, and, following the death of Edward III in June 1377, the process of re-establishing control over Annandale and Teviotdale gathered pace. Indeed, 1378 saw a number of Scottish successes: an unopposed raid came south as far as Hexham; a Scottish fleet sacked Scarborough; the Durham monks were expelled from their cell at Coldingham; and on 25 November a party of Scots seized Berwick, killing its captain, Sir John Boynton. It was quickly recaptured by the new Earl of Northumberland in early December, an event that saw the first appearance in arms of the Earl's heir, Henry Percy, who was only fourteen years old and who, a few years later, would become famous as Hotspur. Two years later, Archibald Douglas raided as far south as Penrith and George Dunbar defeated an English force at Horse Rigg in Northumberland. Little was done by way of counter-attack, much to the Earl's annoyance, basically because the government was anxious to preserve the truce and was therefore prepared to accept Robert II's excuse that he was unable to restrain his Border magnates. There was some, but only some, truth in this; the fact was that Robert II was not unhappy for Douglas and Dunbar to do his work for him, even though they would be the prime beneficiaries.

If the Earl was under restraint from the outset, he became more so between 19 February 1379 and 23 April 1384, during which time Gaunt exercised supreme command on the Border under his commission as King's Lieutenant. His appointment may have been part of a strategy to prevent the Percys and other major Border families, such as the Nevilles, becoming too independently powerful; and to ensure that the government's truce policy was upheld. But it was also a response to the growing authority in southern Scotland of John, Earl of Carrick, Robert II's eldest son: to deal with him required a man of equivalent status and stature. This aspect worked for a time, in that Gaunt's threat to invade kept the Scots quiet from late 1380 until 1383. Then, in the latter year, Wark on Tweed was captured and a raid penetrated twenty miles into Northumberland; and in the following February, the important outpost of Lochmaben fell to the Earl of Douglas, who was then able to complete the recovery of Teviotdale. This signalled an intensification of the war, which was to last until the end of the decade. It was during this time that the Earl's eldest son, Sir Henry Percy (Hotspur), came to the fore.

Gaunt's riposte was a major *chevauchée* into Scotland led by himself and his brother, the Earl of Buckingham. It got as far as Leith, did a great deal of damage, but failed to tempt the Scots into giving battle. This was Gaunt's last contribution to the defence of the Border: on his return to England while staying at Durham he handed over responsibility to defend the Border to the Earl of Northumberland. It has been argued that he was driven to do so by the recognition that, with only the small barony of Embleton, he lacked the power-base to command the Border region of England: defence demanded a Percy. Again, this may only be part of the truth. Gaunt may have tired of his none-too-glamorous role and succumbed to the lure of Castile.

His decision to quit occurred at a dangerous time, since the truce of 1370 had run out in February and had not been renewed. Scottish intentions became clear in November, when a French force under the Admiral of France, Jean de Vienne, landed at Leith to enhance the fighting capacity of the Scottish army. It was intended to be the northern counterpart of a larger French force under the command of Olivier de Clisson, which was to land on the south coast of England. This dual invasion, had it happened, could have had serious consequences. But it did not happen. Instead the English invaded Scotland with a huge army in the summer of 1385. It was Richard II's first campaign, and also the last occasion on which the English government attempted to raise forces by means of the antiquated **feudal levy**. The effort had no spectacular result: as usual, the Scots declined battle and within two weeks the expedition, having reached but not taken Edinburgh, was back in England. However, the size of the English army made it possible for a great deal of damage to be done to southern Scotland, and this helps to explain the almost complete absence of Scottish aggression for the next three years.

All three Percys were fully engaged. The Earl's retinue was the largest, comprising 3 bannerets, 36 knights, 360 esquires and 800 archers; Hotspur had under him 1 banneret, 5 knights, 54 esquires and 60 archers; and Sir Thomas Percy commanded 1 banneret, 13 knights, 66 esquires and 140 archers. The total Percy contribution was 539 men at arms and 1,000 archers and it indicates that collectively the Percys were able to put a small army into the field. The Percy contribution was larger than that of the Constable, the Earl of Buckingham, who was made Duke of Gloucester during this campaign, and only Gaunt, with 1,000 men at arms and 2,000 archers, furnished a larger contingent.

If the Scots were inactive, Hotspur was not. During these years when he was in his early twenties his prowess as a warrior earned him the sobriquet by which he has been known ever since. In fact, it seems clear that, by the second half of the 1380s, it was Hotspur rather than the Earl who was the aggressive force in the defence of the Border. Indeed, the incident in December 1384, when a group of Scots acting without official blessing again seized Berwick, suggests a lack of vigour on the Earl's part. The government clearly thought so, since it severely reprimanded him and he had to undertake to regain the town at his own expense; moreover, this time he did so, not by military action, but by paying the Scots to leave. As we shall see, the Earl was being sidelined by the government and may have been far more concerned with the political than with the military aspect of the Border.

The 1385 invasion resulted in yet another truce, which was to last until 1388. During this interlude Hotspur saw service against the French: he was in the garrison at Calais in 1386, commanded a squadron of ships in the Channel in 1387 and led an expedition that forced the French to abandon the siege of Brest. In 1388, however, he was back on the Border as Warden of the East March (the importance of which is discussed below) at the very large fee of £12,000 a year in time of war. This move was triggered by the refusal of the Scots to renew the truce that expired in February, a sure sign that the renewal of war was imminent. The English government was right to be apprehensive, for the Scottish government was planning a major offensive that it hoped would result in a favourable peace treaty. It was encouraged to think that this was a feasible prospect since England was in a deep political crisis, which is discussed later. Behind this aggressive policy was Robert, Earl of Fife, Robert II's younger son, but the plan had royal support and the army that was assembled was a national force, not merely a gathering of Borderers.

The Scottish strategy is not entirely clear. The original intention may have been to invade the West March with the entire army, secure control of it and then to use it as a diplomatic bargaining counter to obtain a favourable peace treaty. In the event, however, the army divided at Jedburgh, the larger part under the Earl of Fife entering the West March, while the Earls of Douglas and March took their troops into Northumberland. The split may not have been amicable. The two Scottish Border magnates had ambitions of their own to pursue, and they may have been determined to pursue them through an awareness that the English East March defence arrangements were in some disarray as the result of a successful raid in June, in which a large number of Northumbrian gentry were captured. This in turn may have induced the English government to resolve upon another invasion of Scotland led by the king. In preparation for this, orders were issued in July to members of the royal retinue to prepare to join the king's army and to the chief northern lords, including the Earl, to await the arrival of the fleet under the Earl of Arundel.

The Douglas-March invasion ended about a week later with the Battle of Otterburn, famous largely because it became the subject of ballads. These were widespread and popular by the sixteenth century and so must have come into being in some form not long after the event. Unfortunately, they have had the effect of distorting the perception of the event, which they portray as a personal feud between the Douglas and Percy families. Although it is true that both laid claim to the lordship of

The Douglas family

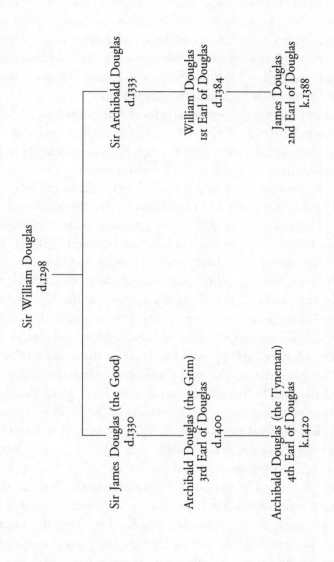

Sir William Douglas
d.1298

Sir Archibald Douglas
d.1333

William Douglas
1st Earl of Douglas
d.1384

James Douglas
2nd Earl of Douglas
k.1388

Sir James Douglas (the Good)
d.1330

Archibald Douglas (the Grim)
3rd Earl of Douglas
d.1400

Archibald Douglas (the Tyneman)
4th Earl of Douglas
k.1420

Jedburgh and Jed Forest, the contemporary evidence does not support this simple interpretation. This is contained in numerous accounts: the chronicle of Jean Froissart, who interviewed participants from both sides within two years of the event; an account by an anonymous monk of Westminster Abbey, who also wrote an account no later than 1391; three Scottish accounts; and in three more written in England, the most interesting being that of John Hardyng, who joined Hotspur's household in 1390 and so must have heard his master's own version.

Because this plethora of versions derived from different sources, each written with its particular bias, certainty as to detail is not possible. What is clear is that the Scottish force swept through Northumberland unopposed, and probably penetrated south of the Tyne to ravage the Brancepeth estate of John, Lord Neville. He was a long-time defender of the Border and a soldier of great competence and experience, but he was close to death (he died on 17 October) and the Scots were probably aware of his incapacity. Meanwhile, Hotspur was in Newcastle, almost certainly with his younger brother, Ralph, then about twenty years old. With him he would have had his own retinue, and it is all but certain that he arrayed the men of the town. Who else was with him is uncertain. Possibly the Northumberland knights Sir Robert and his younger brother Sir Thomas, Umfraville, Sir Robert Ogle, Sir Thomas Grey, and Sir John Lilburn; and also Sir William Hilton from Durham. All of them took part in the battle and all can be identified as members of the Earl's **affinity**. Probably another was Sir Matthew Redman. At first glance this is surprising, given that he was a Westmorland man, but he too was a member of the Earl's affinity and also Captain of Berwick and so subordinate to Hotspur as Warden of the East March. All these men, if present with their retinues, would have given Hotspur a solid professional core to his force.

Douglas and Dunbar appeared before the town, but its defences, comprising a wall twenty feet high and six feet thick fronted by a deep ditch twenty yards broad, were formidable. The Scottish commanders would have known that they had neither the men nor the equipment to mount a successful siege or assault. Assuming they had raided Brancepeth, they would have crossed and then re-crossed the Tyne by the ford at Newburn, from where it required a four-mile detour to reach the walls of

Newcastle. It looks, therefore, as though they were trying to tempt Hotspur into offering battle. He, however, must have felt that his strength was insufficient to respond successfully to the challenge, although there may have been a skirmish outside the walls in which Hotspur's pennant was captured, Froissart's glamourised version of this event should be regarded with suspicion.

After this, the Scots set off on their return journey via Redesdale. Having stormed the tower at Ponteland and captured Sir Aymer de Atholl, they pressed on to Otterburn, where the tower withstood their assault. At this they decided to camp for the night, a few hundred yards north of the village. Hotspur must have had intelligence of their movements, presumably from scouts sent to trail them, since he decided on fast pursuit. What made him move from apparent caution to precipitate action is not clear. One possibility is the very knowledge that the Scots had camped at Otterburn and could, with a swift march, be taken by surprise and also the intelligence that the Bishop of Durham, John Fordham, would soon join him with additional troops. But he must also have realised that were the Scots to escape across the Border without any attempt being made to stop them, he would be accused of being derelict in his duty as Warden of the East March. Whatever his reasons, by means of a forced march he covered the thirty-two miles between Newcastle and Otterburn and caught the Scots off guard.

On what date did this happen? Many versions say the engagement took place on 5 August; others that it was on 19 August. All agree that it took place at night, which makes the latter date more likely in that the new moon rose on 6 August while the full moon occurred on 19 August. An understandable confusion may have arisen from the fact that the former date is St Oswald's day while the latter is St Oswin's day. The 19th is therefore the more likely date.

About the venue there is less doubt: when all the possibilities have been examined, it seems almost certain that fighting took place on the rising ground to the east of the commemorative cross that today stands by the side of the A696, about a mile north of the village. How many men were engaged is another uncertainty. Froissart reckoned that the Scottish force comprised about 400 men at arms and 2,000 infantry, and this is credible, given the size of the Scottish population at that date and that the larger part of their army had gone into the West March. Hotspur's force is said to have been larger, which may explain his willingness to give chase, although it renders less understandable his reluctance to give battle at Newcastle. However, part of his force comprised Newcastle men, whose military competence would have been more amateur than professional.

The precise course of events is all but impossible to discern. It arose, however, from decisions made by Hotspur. One was to attack immediately, even though it was already dusk. This has been seen as another example of his penchant for precipitate action. The chronicler of Westminster Abbey certainly thought so, but this judgement may be unfair. Hotspur's obligation as Warden was to destroy an invading army and relieve it of its booty, and by his rapid advance from Newcastle he had gained that most precious of military advantages, surprise. By morning, that advantage would have gone. And he was aware that three years earlier he had defeated a Scottish force in a night attack as it retreated from an attempt to capture Carlisle. The main consideration in favour of delay was that the arrival of the Durham contingent would give him numerical superiority. It was the sort of finely balanced decision a commander must take under pressure.

His other decision, also open to criticism, was to divide his force, sending Sir Matthew Redman, Sir Thomas and Sir Robert Umfraville and Sir Thomas Grey to circle round behind the Scottish troops and and attack their camp, located several hundred yards further north, in the vicinity of the present Greenchesters Farm. Having successfully done this, they would presumably be expected to regroup and join the main battle, attacking the Scots from the rear. This decision could have had a decisive influence, but initially it meant that Hotspur faced the Scottish force with reduced strength. But the manoeuvre failed: having routed the Scots in the camp, the Redman/Umfraville force chased them towards the Border instead of regrouping and rejoining the main battle, leaving Hotspur under strength.

The battle appears to have been a confused melée lasting until dawn, in which the lack of light and the fact that both armies spoke the same language added to the confusion and uncertainty. What determined the outcome is not clear. The most likely reason is the capture of Hotspur, which would have been a serious psychological blow, as well as depriving the English army of its leader, although in such a kaleidoscopic situation generalship was probably at a discount.

In the end, despite the death of the Earl of Douglas, it was the English who broke. Although the ballads lay emphasis on Douglas's leadership, the presence of George Dunbar, Earl of March should not be forgotten. As his subsequent career showed, he was a very able soldier, and it is possible that he was the more influential of the two leaders. The other factor was the performance of the Bishop of Durham. He and his forces arrived at Newcastle on the morning of 19 August to learn that Hotspur was already heading north in pursuit of the Scots. After pausing for a midday meal, he set off with the intention of joining up with Hotspur, presumably not expecting him to rush immediately into battle. As he neared the scene, he was met by fleeing English troops trying to avoid death or capture. He thereupon decided to retreat to Newcastle rather than to try to retrieve the situation. This too was the sort of decision that a commander has to make on the instant, and he may have done so with the advice of the men with professional knowledge who were with him.

The other unanswered questions are the whereabouts of the Earl and his apparent non-involvement. In part the answer is that in May 1385 he had been removed from the post of Warden, and therefore he had no official role in Border defence. But the more likely reason was that he was one of those who had been ordered to await the arrival of the Admiral, the Earl of Arundel. He may have been in the vicinity; but it is also possible that he was in Yorkshire, where many of his estates were located and where he had official duties. And to exonerate him from the charge of wilful neglect, some of the most prominent members of his affinity were serving with Hotspur.

What was the balance sheet of the battle? For the English, it was the first and only occasion when they were defeated on their own soil by the Scots in a major engagement. More immediately, the loss of Hotspur was considered so serious that the Commons agreed that £3,000 of the current **subsidy** should be devoted to his ransom, payment of which secured his release by October. But the loss of knights, set by one chronicler at twenty-one, including Hotspur's seriously wounded brother, Ralph, was also a severe blow in two senses: it depleted the defence capability of the Border and the cost of their ransoms was a drain on the resources of the region. Added to this was a very considerable loss of life. Numbers quoted by the chroniclers vary, but most claimed that the death toll exceeded 1,000. This was all but confirmed in 1877, when the skeletal remains of 1,200 mostly young and middle-aged men were found during renovations under the north wall of the nave of Elsdon church, a part of the building that was built around 1400. Although five miles from the site of the battle, this church was the correct burial place, since it was then the parish church for that part of Redesdale.

For the Scots it was a notable victory, albeit one marred by the death of Douglas. Their other losses are not recorded in as much detail as those of the English, but they must have been heavy during the battle, although far less in the pursuit, when defeated armies usually suffered most of their casualties. And, of course, they were able to return to Scotland with their booty and ransomable prisoners, which for many was the true purpose of the expedition. But, for the Scottish government, the gains were almost nil. Although Northumberland's defences were so depleted that in the following June a major raid got as far south as Tynemouth, the county was not totally vulnerable. Sir Matthew Redman and Sir Robert Ogle, two men who had avoided capture at Otterburn, were able to field a sufficient force to maul the Scottish rearguard quite badly as it returned home. More serious was the Anglo-French truce, agreed on 18 June, which made further Scottish aggression a high-risk strategy as it was almost certain to provoke a major invasion by an English government no longer distracted by a war with France. The war was effectively over in the summer of 1389, leaving the Scottish Crown empty handed: Berwick was still in English hands; and the English king had not been driven to abandon his claim to the lordship of Scotland. As regards the internal politics of Scotland, the death of the Earl of Douglas had profound repercussions in that the Earl of Carrick's power was rapidly eroded and the role of Governor of Scotland was granted to his younger brother, Robert, Earl of Fife.

In 1388, Hotspur was the man in command, but two earlier episodes in his military career tell something of his apprentice days as a fighting knight. Both took place in 1383, when he was nineteen, and both had a crusading aspect. The first was a visit to Prussia. It is a pity that we do not have the details of this venture, as we do for those of Gaunt's son, Henry of Bolingbroke, who twice went there, in 1390 and 1392. That of 1390 was financed by Gaunt, whose wealth enabled the expedition to be equipped on such a lavish scale that two ships were required to transport Boling-broke, his retainers and his servants from Boston to Rixhoft. The whole adventure lasted nine months, from late July 1390 until the end of April 1391. Bolingbroke and his fellow knights took part in the campaign of the year conducted by the Teutonic Knights, in which one of their number was killed. But apart from the serious business, there was much time for the usual aristocratic pastimes of tournaments and feasts.

Hotspur's father, although wealthy, would not have been able to finance such a lavish expedition for his son. Consequently, it is likely that Hotspur went with a group of young knights and esquires. The aims of such men were various, but material gain cannot have been one of them, for there was none to be had from the primitive inhabitants of the forests and marshes of Samogitia. But as such ventures were classified as crusades, participants could convince themselves that they would gain spiritual benefit, although this was probably not a major consideration. Uppermost in their minds was the knowledge that participation in a *reise* had cult status: to take part and perform with well-reported skill and bravery would guarantee an enhanced reputation within the ranks of the knightly class. Not for nothing did Chaucer have his Knight take part not only in a *reise* in *Pruce* (Prussia), but also to fight in Spain and North Africa, two other areas where the enemies of Christendom were to be found. In going to the Baltic, Hotspur was very much in tune with the spirit and values of his age.

His visit, however, appears to have been cut short, for he was recalled in order to take part in what is known as the Norwich Crusade, which was a scandalous event based upon an abuse of the crusading idea and ideal. What brought it about was a combination of disparate circumstances. The train of events began in 1382 with the revolt of the people of the important cloth-making town of Ghent against their ruler, Louis de Maele, Count of Flanders, whom they defeated on 3 May at Beverhoutsveld. Because of the importance of the Flemish towns to England's wool exports and thereby to

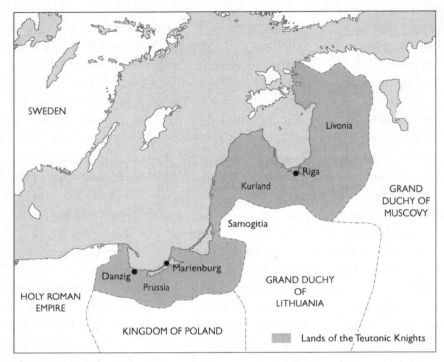

Baltic Crusades

the royal income, the political situation in Flanders was of vital interest. There was also a strategic aspect. Louis de Maele's heir, his daughter, Margaret, was married to the French king's uncle, Philippe, Duke of Burgundy. When Philippe succeeded his father-in-law as Count, Flanders would become firmly aligned with France. There was every reason, therefore, for England to intervene on the side of the Gantois. If this could be done successfully, England might extend its line of coastal 'barbicans' northwards from Calais.

There were two problems, however. One was that an expedition to Flanders would compete with Gaunt's plans to invade Castile in pursuit of his claim to the throne. The other was finance: how to raise the money to pay for an expeditionary force of sufficient size, when the Commons were reluctant to increase the tax burden? The solution, made possible by the Great Schism, was to declare the expedition a crusade: both Urban VI and Clement VII had declared that action against the other pope could be so classified.

Since England had opted for Urban, while France supported Clement, any English action against France might qualify for crusading status. The only difficulty was that the proposed action was to be against the Count of Flanders, who also recognised Urban VI. This was dismissed as irrelevant, however, since it was argued that the King of France was the overlord of the Count of Flanders and in any case the succession of the Duke of Burgundy as Count would automatically bring Flanders into the Clementist camp.

The situation became urgent in November with the defeat of the Gantois by a French army at Roosebeke and the subsequent occupation of Bruges. The circumstance was ideal for the aristocratic and warlike Henry Despenser, Bishop of Norwich. Late in 1382 he set about raising an army of 2,500 men at arms and 2,500 archers, to pay for which he had papal authority to offer remission of sins to all who either took part or contributed financially. The response was enthusiastic, and the money garnered by his collectors, who were accompanied by friars, when added to a small grant from the Exchequer, was sufficient to mount the expedition.

The adventure, which began when the army landed at Calais on 17 May and lasted until October, was an unmitigated fiasco. Initially, progress was promising with the capture or surrender of a series of coastal towns: Gravelines, Dunkirk, Nieuport, Dixmude and Blankenberge. But then Despenser allowed himself to be persuaded by the Gantois to besiege Ypres, a task for which his army was not equipped. The failure to take Ypres and the approach of a large French army commanded by the Duke of Burgundy led to the whole enterprise being aborted and to the trial of Despenser on his return to England. Hotspur was a member of this expedition, but there is no record of the part he played. The fact that he was not yet twenty makes it doubtful that he had a position of command.

Politics

In the twenty-one years between 1368 and 1389 there were three major national political crises that disrupted the functioning of government and to differing extents threatened the Crown. Members of the Percy family were involved in all of them to some degree, but for the Earl and his son there was a more urgent concern, namely the control and management of

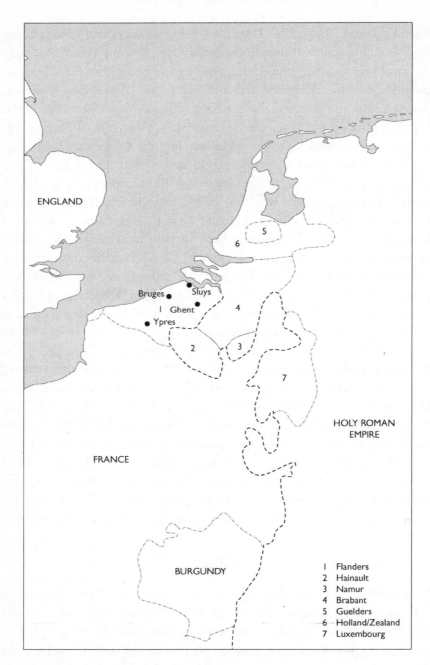

ENGLAND

5

6

Bruges ● ● Sluys

1 Ghent ●

● Ypres

4

2

3

7

HOLY ROMAN
EMPIRE

FRANCE

BURGUNDY

1 Flanders
2 Hainault
3 Namur
4 Brabant
5 Guelders
6 Holland/Zealand
7 Luxembourg

The Low Countries and Burgundy

the Border region through the office of Warden of the Marches. This had come into existence as a response to the permanence of hostilities between England and Scotland and had evolved to achieve its final form by the middle of the fourteenth century. While these two matters were never unconnected, they need to be discussed separately.

The first of the major crises spanned the last months of Edward III's reign, the death of his heir, the Black Prince, and the first months of the reign of his ten-year-old grandson, Richard II. The underlying cause was the absence of an adult and fully effective king. By 1376, Edward III was fast becoming incapable of action and pathetically dependent upon his mistress, the grasping and unscrupulous Alice Perrers. His heir, who might have taken over the exercise of kingship, died in June 1376. As a result, it was virtually certain that in the near future the Crown would pass to a child, the Black Prince's son, Richard. This would be prevented only by Richard's sudden death; or by the usurpation of his uncle, John of Gaunt, now the eldest of Edward III's sons, a possibility that crossed some minds. Gaunt, in fact, was the central figure in this crisis.

The crisis began with the opening of what came to be known as the 'Good Parliament' on 28 April 1376. As always, the reason for its calling was the government's financial need that could be met only by the grant of a subsidy. The reaction of the Commons was implacable hostility: no fewer than 146 petitions were presented, the contents of which revealed the range and depth of concern among the lesser members of the political nation about the government's performance. In brief, these amounted to bitter complaints about the government's failure to prosecute the war successfully, extravagance and embezzlement of public funds and the corruption and inefficiency of government, locally and centrally. The feelings of the Commons were presented by one of its members, Sir Peter de la Mare, one of the knights from Herefordshire, chosen, it is said, because of his proven ability to present the case succinctly and forcefully. This incident is traditionally taken to mark the origins of the office of Speaker. To determine suitable remedies, de la Mare asked for a meeting of members of the Commons with twelve members of the Lords.

Behind this apparent detached concern for good government lay more partisan political considerations. De la Mare was the steward of Edmund

Mortimer, Earl of March, whose name headed the list of twelve peers chosen to help find remedies for the nation's ills. March's wife was Philippa, the only child of Lionel, Duke of Clarence, Edward III's second son and therefore, until his premature death in 1368, the elder brother of John of Gaunt. If succession through the female were not debarred, offspring of Philippa's marriage would take precedence over Gaunt and his son, Henry of Bolingbroke. It would seem, therefore, that there was something of a power struggle, or at least a manoeuvring for position, with a view to what might be the situation after the deaths of Edward III and the Black Prince.

Where was Henry, Lord Percy in all this? As kin by marriage to Gaunt, with whom he had grown up and with whom he had been closely associated in the French wars, political alliance with the Duke of Lancaster would seem to have been natural and logical. Yet he was one of the twelve lords chosen to treat with the Commons, which hints at an association with the March faction. As if to confirm this, before the end of 1379, Percy's heir, Henry, the future Hotspur, was married to March's daughter, Elizabeth. When this was first mooted between the respective fathers is not known, but it is likely that they were discussing the possibility at the time of the 1376 crisis. And Percy does seem to have been considered as an active supporter of the Commons during the summer of 1376. It was during this session that the Commons accidentally invented the process of impeachment: the collective accusation by the Commons against a member of the government, who was then tried by the Lords. By means of this device, they succeeded in getting rid of the leading members of the royal household, notably the Chamberlain, William, Lord Latimer, and the Steward, John, Lord Neville, and replacing certain members of the Council with new men, including Percy.

The triumph of the Commons was short lived. To Gaunt, who never wavered in his belief in the royal prerogative, their almost unbelievable temerity in forcing changes on the Crown was an unwarrantable and intolerable insult, and in the months that followed the closing of Parliament in July he engineered a counter-coup. Peter de la Mare was imprisoned, the Acts of the summer's Parliament were annulled, Alice Perrers, who had been driven from court, was allowed to return, and Lord Latimer was reinstated. Moreover, on the death of the Black Prince, his son, Richard, was proclaimed Prince of Wales, Duke of Cornwall and Earl of Chester, the honours normally awarded to the heir-apparent to the throne, a prompt action designed to scotch rumours of his intention to seize the throne. But above all, Gaunt went for William Wykeham, Bishop of Winchester, who had been prominent in the impeachment of Lord Latimer. Charging him with malversation during his time as Chancellor, which had ended as long ago as 1371, he secured a conviction with the confiscation of his temporalities as punishment. During these weeks the Earl of March was bullied into stepping down as Marshal and the post was given to Lord Percy, possibly as a bribe to secure his change of adherence.

It was as Marshal and an ally of Gaunt that Percy was heavily involved in the politics of the following months. These were very much concerned with Gaunt's quarrel with the Church triggered by his treatment of Wykeham. But it did not end there, for Gaunt hired the services of the Oxford scholar, John Wycliffe, to preach around London his controversial, but by no means unpopular, arguments against the wealth and worldly concerns of the upper echelons of the Church. However, the Church was not so easily cowed. It had in William Courtenay, Bishop of London, a son of the Earl of Devon, a man whose aristocratic background and masterful temperament gave him the necessary confidence to stand up to Gaunt in the defence of the wealth and privileges of his order.

The crisis came in February 1377. A new Parliament met, one completely responsive to Gaunt's wishes; but Convocation, meeting at the same time and with the same purpose, namely, to grant taxation, was not so pliant. Wykeham was not present when the meeting opened, and Courtenay refused to allow it to proceed until he had taken his seat. Courtenay followed up this initial success by summoning Wycliffe to appear before the bishops on 19 February at St Paul's Cathedral to answer charges concerning his theological opinions. Gaunt took up the challenge, hiring four trained theologians, one from each of the mendicant orders, to assist in Wycliffe's defence. When the day came, Gaunt and Percy with their armed retinues escorted Wycliffe through the crowds and into St Paul's, Percy brandishing his Marshal's baton. Whether intended or not, this act was very provocative in that the City of London and the precincts of the cathedral were outside the Marshal's jurisdiction. A violent quarre developed about this and Courtenay's refusal to allow the accused to be seated, with the result that the trial was abandoned in uproar.

From this moment the concerns of Londoners began to play a crucial part. Rumours that Percy was about to use his authority as Marshal to impose control upon the City began to spread, fuelled by a story that he had imprisoned a citizen in his prison, the Marshalsea. This was duly stormed and the man released. The mob then converged on Gaunt's London residence, the Savoy Palace. Fortunately for the duke and Percy, they were not there but at the house of one of Gaunt's supporters, Sir John Ypres. There they were tipped off by one of Gaunt's retinue and in panic left the dinner and fled across the Thames to find refuge with the Black Prince's widow, Joan, at Kennington Palace.

In the following days, tempers cooled and the City of London was driven to make a humiliating peace with Gaunt. Although his actions regained Gaunt the political initiative, he displayed an aristocratic hauteur and an unbending assurance of the rightness of his position, combined with a disdain for the concerns of those he was intent on browbeating. It was an impolitic and not very pretty performance, and it served to earn him the deep and abiding hatred of Londoners.

Percy's alliance with Gaunt continued until the death of Edward III and the coronation of Richard II. The old king died on 21 June and the coronation of his young grandson was arranged for 16 July. In their respective roles, Gaunt as hereditary Steward of England and Percy as Marshal were responsible for much of the ceremonial. The two men headed the traditional procession from the Tower to Westminster the day before the coronation, and took prominent roles at the feast that followed the ceremony. It was on the occasion of the coronation that Percy was elevated to the earldom of Northumberland, together with the king's youngest uncle, Thomas of Woodstock, who became Earl of Buckingham, Thomas Mowbray, who was made Earl of Nottingham and one of the king's tutors, Guichard d'Angle, who became Earl of Huntingdon. How these elevations were arranged and by whom is not clear, but we must assume that Percy's elevation was the consequence of his alliance with Gaunt. It seemed, therefore, that Gaunt was to be the dominant figure in the politics of the new king's juvenile years, with Percy as a major supporter.

But appearances were deceptive. In the days that followed the corona-tion, a Grand Council, formed to determine how the country should be governed during the minority, selected twelve members to form the standing council to act in the young king's name. The composition of this body reveals a sudden change in the political climate: prominent by their presence were Edmund Mortimer, Third Earl of March and Bishop Courtenay, together with his episcopal colleague and ally, Ralph Erghum of Salisbury, and, by their absence, Gaunt and Percy. Gaunt, in fact, surrendered Hertford Castle and withdrew from court. It was clear that the death of his father had significantly reduced his authority. And as Gaunt's standing declined, so did Percy's: he resigned, willingly or otherwise, the office of Marshal, which went to Sir John Fitzalan, the brother of the Earl of Arundel.

In the four years that followed, the former allies were to become seriously estranged. The process began in February 1379 with Gaunt's appointment as King's Lieutenant in the North, with wide-ranging powers to deal with Border defence and negotiations with the Scots. This meant that during the term of his commission, Gaunt had the authority to appoint all the Wardens, who would be answerable to him. His base for this role was the small Northumberland barony of Embleton, with its mighty castle at Dunstanburgh built by his first wife's uncle, Thomas, Earl of Lancaster. It could not be argued that there was no case for this arrangement and for his appointment, since the previous year had seen much raiding and counter-raiding, including the temporary loss of Berwick in late November. More urgently, only royal personages such as Gaunt and his Scottish counterpart, the Earl of Carrick, had sufficient status to speak for their respective governments. For the Earl, however, this was a blow to his undoubted ambition to become the dominant force in the English Border region. This would be secured by three means. The first had been accomplished. By acquiring the title of earl, he had placed himself on a higher plane than his potential rivals such as John, Lord Neville of Raby, and Roger, Lord Clifford of Brougham. The second was the enlargement of his estate, a process on which he had embarked through his arrangement with Gilbert Umfraville, Earl of Angus and which would be completed when he married Umfraville's widow in 1381. The third was permanently to hold the wardenship of the Marches. This would give him authority as well as power and provide him with an additional income in the form of the fees of office with which he would be able to maintain an enlarged retinue. The history of the appointments to the wardenships of the East and West Marches is discussed below. What needs to be recognised here is that the creation of the role of King's Lieutenant and the appointment of Gaunt looked set to thwart this strand of his ambition.

Gaunt remained in charge of Border matters until 1384, but in that period the second major political crisis blew up in which both the Earl and his brother Thomas were involved. This was the uprisings in the summer of 1381, to which the collective name of 'the Peasants' Revolt' has been applied. This is a not very helpful title, particularly as the word 'peasant' now has pejorative overtones and does not convey the social and occupational diversity of the participants. In fact, the locations of many of the events of these weeks were towns and many of the issues were urban in character. Many who took part, and many of the leaders, were craftsmen rather than tenant farmers or farm labourers, and in some places they secured gentry support. Moreover, while the communistic notions preached by such men as the priest John Ball were no doubt widely attractive and probably long held, the demand for the abolition of **serfdom** and the wage control legislation of 1351 would be real and urgent, but only where they were relevant, which was not everywhere. In fact, the target(s) of each group of the rebels was, or were, specific. Most notable were certain monasteries, which in estate management were conspicuously conservative and unresponsive to changing conditions; lawyers, who were seen as agents of the controlling classes; and certain figures in government, particularly John of Gaunt. Overall, the contentious issues in the uprisings were primarily local and only secondarily universal. And serious trouble was confined to nine counties. Of these, the most severely affected were in the south-east: Kent, Essex, Cambridge, Norfolk, Suffolk, Bedford and Buckingham. In addition, there were disturbances in Somerset and in two northern counties, Cheshire and Yorkshire. Thirteen towns were seriously disturbed: London, St Albans, Bury St Edmunds, Cambridge, Ely, Peterborough, Lowestoft, Norwich, Salisbury, Winchester, York,

Beverley and Scarborough. Although widespread, and revealing the ease with which rebels in various areas communicated with each other, the uprising was far from ubiquitous, many areas of the country experiencing little or no disturbance.

The revolt was sparked by the third **poll tax**, the novel form of taxation introduced in 1377, ordered by Parliament late in 1380. This time, in contrast to the two previous occasions, there were no gradations and, to make matters worse, the rate per head was tripled from 4d (2p) to 1s (5p). Inevitably, there was widespread resentment and extensive evasion, but it was the heavy-handed methods used to try to enforce payment that provoked the explosion. Violent reactions occurred almost simultaneously in the first days of June in Essex and Kent, and almost at once the rebels in the two counties were in touch with each other. On Thursday, 13 June there was an inconclusive meeting between the king and the Kentish rebels at Blackheath, but later that day the authorities lost control of the situation when London Bridge and its gate were opened (by whom is not known) and the rebels occupied the city. For the next few hours, the situation was out of control. The Fleet and Newgate prisons were liberated and the Temple (occupied by the hated lawyers) and the Preceptory of the Knights of St John at Clerkenwell were sacked. Most notable was the total destruction of the Savoy Palace, Gaunt's London home. Such was the hatred of him in the capital that the building was demolished and all Gaunt's possessions were consigned to the flames or the Thames.

The following day, Friday, the situation deteriorated. The king again met the rebels, now led by the charismatic Kentishman, Wat Tyler, this time at Mile End. There he agreed to the abolition of serfdom and a standard rent for land of 4d (2p), per acre. This failed to defuse the crisis, however. Some of the rebels managed to get into the Tower, where they murdered the Archbishop of Canterbury, Simon Sudbury, and the Treasurer, Sir Robert Hales, and elsewhere in the city massacred an unknown number of foreigners.

The crisis came to a head the next day, Saturday 15 June, at a third meeting between the king and the rebel host. Since the royal party included 200 or more men at arms, it seems likely that government was recovering its nerve and was intent on a showdown. The venue was

Smithfield. Accounts of what happened vary considerably in detail, but all are agreed that there was an altercation that led to Tyler, whose actions and attitude were apparently insolent and provocative, being struck down by the Mayor of London, Sir William Walworth. This could have provoked disaster and it is far from clear why it did not. The story that the young king spurred his horse forward, declared to the rebels that he would now be their leader and agreed to all of their demands is attractive and may be true, although it does smack of royalist propaganda. Whatever did happen, Tyler's death deflated the rebellion and allowed the court and the city authorities to regain control of London, although it was not until the following month that the last embers of the rebellion were stamped out.

Throughout the crisis in and on the edge of London, Thomas Percy was a member of the entourage protecting the boy king. Since he is known to have been at the meeting with the rebels at Mile End, it is likely that he was among the group of nobles with the king throughout the crisis, including the meeting at Smithfield. The probable reason was his close association with the king's youngest uncle, Thomas of Woodstock, Earl of Buckingham, with whom he had campaigned in Brittany in 1377 and 1380. It was to Buckingham that a wide-ranging commission was issued to suppress the uprising and it was he and Percy who applied the necessary force to snuff out the revolt in Essex, the most militant county. The opportunity arose during the pacifying and punitive visit to Essex towards the end of June by the king and the Chief Justice of the King's Bench, Sir Robert Tresilian. When the royal party reached Waltham on the 22nd they were approached by a deputation of the rebels, who demanded the confirmation of the reforms the king had granted a few days earlier. Needless to say, now that the back of the revolt had been broken, they got a negative answer. Their response was renewed resistance. By the 27th, a large number of rebels had gathered and created a fortified *laager* of carts alongside a wood near Billericay. The following day, however, they were easily dispersed by the men at arms commanded by Buckingham and Percy, who chased them as far as Sudbury and Colchester. This cleared the way for Tresilian to conduct a thorough repression of rebellion in the county.

Both before and after this, Percy was also involved in the uprising of the tenants of St Albans Abbey. On 16 June, he and the Steward of the

Household, Sir Hugh Seagrave, were at St Albans, where they advised the abbot, Thomas de la Mare, to give in to the rebel demands, on the understanding that any concessions could be withdrawn once control had been restored. This became possible three weeks later. On 6 July, Percy and the Earl of Warwick were ordered to suppress the St Albans revolt. Warwick, however, was diverted by a crisis on his own estates, and order was restored when the king himself came to St Albans on 12 July. It is probable that Thomas Percy was a member of the royal entourage.

Meanwhile, the Earl was at the other end of the country, at Alnwick, about his business as Warden of the East March. His erstwhile ally, Gaunt, was fifteen miles further north at Berwick, from where on 18 June he went to meet the Earl of Carrick at Ebchester, near Ayton, two miles up the Tweed, to arrange a truce. He was fortunate in being so far from London, otherwise it is possible he would have been murdered. Having heard the news of the uprising and declined an offer from the Scots to help with its suppression, he returned to Berwick. Three days later he moved south, heading for the Earl's castle at Alnwick, when he was intercepted by two of the Earl's retinue, Sir John Hotham and Thomas Motherby. As a result of their conversation, Gaunt at once turned north, sought and received a safe conduct from the Earl of Carrick, and crossed into Scotland. Unfortunately, we do not know what the Earl's messengers said, but it was enough to panic Gaunt into flight. What they should have told him was that a message had been received from the Earl of Stafford and the Bishop of Hereford in London that the situation there was uncertain and that Gaunt should stay at Bamburgh until it was safe to return to the capital.

Gaunt remained in Scotland as an honoured guest throughout most of July and returned to London only on receipt of letters from the king. His mood, however, was bitter. No doubt angered by the loss of the Savoy Palace and its contents and by rumours that he had fled to Scotland through cowardice, Gaunt vented his spleen on the Earl, accusing him of denying him protection and spreading the allegation that his relations with the Scots were treasonous. These accusations were made at the meetings of the council at Reading on 4 August and at Westminster on the 15th. On the latter occasion Gaunt challenged the Earl to combat by throwing down his glove and it required the intervention of the king and several earls to get

Gaunt to cool down. On both occasions, the Earl appears to have acted with restraint, merely denying Gaunt's accusations. But when Gaunt renewed his accusations at another meeting of the royal council, this time at Berkhamstead, on 9 October, the Earl exploded with a torrent of abuse against his tormentor, apparently in strong northern dialect rather than French. By this failure of self-control in the presence of the king, he was guilty of *lese-majesté*. Consequently he was arrested, but then released on sureties of two fellow earls that he would appear before Parliament when it met the following month.

The matter became more serious as both men came to Westminster for the parliamentary session with armed retinues. Being an enemy of Gaunt made the Earl hugely popular with Londoners, who proclaimed their support by conferring citizenship upon him. When the issue was raised, Gaunt repeated his accusations, but on this occasion the Earl produced the letter, which he believed would vindicate him, and it became clear that the misunderstanding had arisen from the actions of his messengers. Although it was the Earl who had been falsely accused, it was he who, on the urging of the king, had to beg forgiveness. Next day in full Parliament the Earl on his knees begged both the king and Gaunt for pardon and for the latter's good lordship, acknowledging him to be 'the greatest lord and most exalted person in the realm after my liege lord the king'. The Earl and Gaunt then exchanged the kiss of peace, with which the incident was formally closed.

It seems clear that Gaunt had not been willing to let the matter drop until he had humiliated the Earl. To that end, and perhaps with clear intent, he provoked the Earl into losing his temper and using intemperate language in a situation where that could not be excused. What little we know of the Earl's character does not suggest that it was of the purest; but on this occasion he does appear to have been the wronged party. Gaunt was, as on previous occasions, unbendingly jealous of his honour and his royal status and quick to react to any perceived slight upon them. Through his ability to occupy and retain the upper ground, he had been able to humiliate the Earl, but his performance lacked the magnanimity looked for in a prince.

Long after this resolution had been achieved, the Earl was involved briefly in the aftermath of the rebellion in Yorkshire. In that county there had been three uprisings, all in towns – York, Beverley and Scarborough – and all provoked by internal tensions arising from tight oligarchic control. That at Scarborough began on 23 June and was a popular uprising against the five families who controlled the town, led by three men, two of whom were wealthy, but excluded from power. The Earl's role was to head the justices who sat in the town on 26 August 1382 to hear evidence and determine punishment, which was an amercement set at 900 marks (£600).

The final aspect of the political manoeuvrings of these years brings us back to the Border and in particular to the wardenships of the Marches. There is little doubt that the Earl wished to secure these offices for himself and his son. By doing so the Percys would gain income in the form of fees of office, but also the standing and prestige that would enable him to attract men to their affinities. Although the fees varied with each fresh commission and between peace and war, they were considerable and, assuming they were paid, could increase the family income several fold. For example, in October 1399, the East March fees were set at £3,000 in peace and £12,000 in war, while the West March carried fees of £1,500 and £6,000. Admittedly, these were exceptionally high in an exceptional circumstance, but they serve to underline the advantage that accrued from the wardenships. This enhanced power and resources would then make easier the pursuit of potential family interests on or north of the Border. It was this potential for independent action that the government in Westminster disliked and mistrusted. In particular, they were concerned that a man like the Earl would not scruple to use his power and authority to pursue aims that were contrary to its own, which was the maintenance of the truce. The Crown was not prepared to see a Percy in England have the freedom of action that a Douglas or a Dunbar enjoyed in Scotland.

This is the concern that lay behind the creation of the office of King's Lieutenant and the appointment of Gaunt in 1379. Until he relinquished the role in 1384, it is clear that there was a struggle between Gaunt and the Earl, with the latter striving to hold on to some vestige of power. The advent of Gaunt had an immediate effect. Since 1377, the Earl had been, jointly with others, Warden of the East March and the West March. In

June of that year, however, he was removed from the West March and in December from the East March as well. In March 1380, he was restored to the East March, but his tenure lasted only until December 1381, when, doubtless as a consequence of their quarrel, Gaunt replaced him with someone more congenial, John, Lord Neville of Raby, a longstanding member of his affinity. Against this the Earl protested with sufficient vigour to force a compromise: the East March was divided in two by the creation of a Middle March. This was to be that part of Northumberland between the West March and the Newcastle–Roxburgh road. If this was roughly the present A696 and A68, it put the Earl's bases at Alnwick and Warkworth within Neville's jurisdiction: Gaunt was rubbing salt into the wound. This arrangement lasted until March 1382, when the Earl and Neville were made joint wardens of both marches. The Earl's restoration was very brief: three months later, in June, the East March was again divided, although this time the Earl's jurisdiction also included the land around Alnwick and Warkworth.

Then, between March and May 1383, the Earl suffered the indignity of being entirely out of office and seeing John Neville installed as warden of both marches. But in May of that year, he was restored to the large commission that was responsible for the entire Border, an arrangement that lasted only until August, when he was removed in favour of his brother, Thomas, who served alongside Neville. At the beginning of 1384, he was again added to the commission, a situation that continued until July, when Hotspur replaced his uncle, Thomas.

Gaunt's decision in April 1384 to abandon the cold of the Border for the warmth of Spain and Portugal must have been a considerable relief to the Earl, since his tormentor of 1381 had become a permanent bugbear. In the months immediately following Gaunt's departure, the situation seemed to return to normal, with the Earl's appointment in August 1384 as Warden of the East March and joint Warden of the West March. His contract lasted until May 1385, when he was removed, in favour of his son, Hotspur. That Richard II's government intended to continue Gaunt's policy of denying the Percy's complete control of the Border became fully apparent in April 1386, when Hotspur was stood down and John Neville was made sole Warden of the East March as well as continuing as joint Warden of the

West March. This remained the situation until June 1388, when Hotspur was reappointed as Warden of the East March. The reason for his recall was almost certainly because of Neville's failing health, not because he was a Percy. Moreover, the appointment of John, Lord Beaumont, a man without any interests in the Border region, to be Warden of the West March, indicated that the Crown was not prepared to abandon its policy of thwarting Percy ambitions in the Border zone.

The third political crisis was the most prolonged, lasting from October 1386 until June 1388. And it was the most serious in that at one stage Richard II came close to being deposed. Its genesis lay in the young king's partiality and lack of political perspicacity, which was manifest in his reliance upon certain individuals on whom he lavished lands and titles. The most prominent was Robert de Vere, Earl of Oxford, an attractive young man a few years older than Richard, but almost entirely lacking worth and wisdom and concerned primarily with the enlargement of his estate. Yet he was very evidently the king's favourite, so much so that Richard bestowed on him the titles Marquis of Dublin in 1385 and then in the following year Duke of Ireland, with full palatine powers. These moves provoked feelings of outrage within the ranks of the nobility: not only had the title of marquis never previously been used in England, but it gave its holder precedence over all the earls; while the title of duke, first granted in 1337, was hitherto confined to the royal family.

The hostile reaction to de Vere's elevation was justified and understandable, since he was unworthy, in either ability or experience, of the titles and powers granted to him. But the two other men most closely associated with Richard were of an older generation, of proven ability and had served Richard's father and grandfather with distinction. One was Sir Michael de la Pole, the son of a wealthy Hull merchant, Sir William de la Pole, whose financial acumen had helped Edward III to raise money for his campaigns in France. Richard elevated him to the peerage in 1385 as Earl of Suffolk, despite Pole's incompetent performance as Chancellor since 1383, in particular, his failure to implement agreed financial reforms and his lack of vigour in preparing the country's defences against a French invasion. The Suffolk title had fallen into the Crown's hand on the death without heirs of its previous holder. In conferring it, Richard was entirely within his rights, but it was resented as Pole was regarded as a *parvenu*. Moreover, not only were his and de Vere's elevations disliked for particular reasons, they also raised concern in that they were not done in parliament, as was the case in Edward III's reign.

The other older man was Sir Simon Burley, the king's tutor, a longtime companion in arms of Richard's father, the Black Prince, and a man with a distinguished military record. He too, like de Vere, was desperate to increase his wealth by acquiring land, and was not above using dubious means to achieve his ends. But his interests were also intellectual, including a particular interest in the theories and practice of kingship, in which he may have instructed his royal charge.

There were also several younger and less important members of the royal household and one particular member of the London elite, Sir Nicholas Brembre, to whom Richard looked to control the city in the royal interest. Given the fact that he was still in his teens, it is not surprising that Richard felt a deep need for the support of people he liked or looked up to. This said, however, it is clear that he was deeply conscious of, as he saw it, the divinely bestowed royal prerogative. What he failed to appreciate was that the English political process was consensual: the exercise of royal power was not a simple matter of command and obedience, but required skilful and even-handed co-operation with other members of the political nation.

However, none of his actions was clearly wrong or unconstitutional. What made them risky was their political partiality, which aroused the resentment of a group of powerful nobles, who felt excluded from what they considered to be their rightful place in the social and political order. The leading figure was the king's youngest uncle, Thomas of Woodstock, who was made Earl of Buckingham at Richard's coronation in 1377, and then Duke of Gloucester on the occasion of Richard's expedition into Scotland in 1385. With his older brother, Gaunt, away in Spain, Gloucester had a clear field to promote his own interests. Closely associated with him were two brothers, Richard Fitzalan, Earl of Arundel and Thomas Arundel, Bishop of Ely, and also Thomas Beauchamp, Earl of Warwick. Their resentments were various. As regards foreign policy, they recognised that Richard favoured peace with France, while they were for a more

A scene from the jousts at St Inglevert,
from a fifteenth-century copy of Jean Froissart's
Chronicles (British Library MS Harley
4379, f.23v)

The Earl of Northumberland taking an
oath to Richard II *Chronicles* (British Library
MS Harley 1319, f.41v)

Richard II betrayed by the Earl of Northumberland
(British Library MS Harley 1319, f.37v)

Richard II receiving the Earl of Northumberland at
Conway Castle (British Library MS Harley 1319, f.44)

Richard II surrenders the crown to Henry
(British Library MS Harley 4380, f.184v)

Richard of Warwick is invested with the Order of the
Garter on the field of Shrewsbury in 1403 (British
Library, MS Cotton Julius E IV, art.6, f.4v)

vigorous prosecution of the war. In this they were genuine and could rely on the support of many of the lesser landowners for whom fighting in France was the means of wealth enhancement. At home, they alleged that the king's ministers and members of his household were guilty of inefficiency and corruption, a charge with a good foundation. But beneath their expressed concern for honest government and a forward foreign policy was a basic desire to control the young king in their own interests. Gloucester in particular almost certainly harboured a longstanding resentment at his modest endowment compared with that of his brothers, which was heightened by Richard's lavish generosity towards de Vere.

The crisis began when Parliament met at the beginning of October 1386. The Commons were in recalcitrant mood and fully at one with the king's opponents on the subject of corruption in high places. Being so, they refused to vote taxation and demanded the removal of de la Pole from office. Gloucester and Bishop Arundel went to see Richard at Eltham with this demand. Richard reacted angrily, going so far as to hint that he might be prepared to ask the King of France for support. This produced an equally strong response from Gloucester, who reminded Richard of the fate of his great-grandfather, Edward II. Richard, who would have been aware of this and of the obvious comparison between de Vere and Piers Gaveston, Edward II's favourite, backed down.

Having made this breakthrough, Gloucester and his friends took control of the government. De la Pole was removed from office and impeached and replaced by Bishop Arundel, and a fourteen-man commission was set up to scrutinise the king's finances and supervise the running of his household. These were challenging, although not unprecedented, moves. Richard, however, slipped out of their immediate grasp by leaving the London area and going on a tour of counties on the Welsh border and in the north Midlands. Apart from the need to escape the physical clutches of Gloucester, he wished to assure himself of a military power base in the royal county of Cheshire. And he also took the opportunity of consulting the chief justices concerning the legality of what was happening in Westminster. Their responses at meetings at Shrewsbury and Nottingham, although radical enough for his liking, were high risk and confrontational, if adopted as the basis for action. The judges' opinion was that not only did the commission contravene the king's prerogative, but those responsible were traitors. In so saying, they extended the meaning of treason well beyond the close definition set down in the Statute of Treasons in 1352. It is clear that Richard intended to keep these opinions secret, presumably no doubt to be able to bring them into play at a moment of his own choosing. But they were leaked to Gloucester and his associates, who thereby became aware of the king's strategy. Richard also wrote to the sheriffs, hoping to persuade them to contrive the return of sympathetic members of Parliament. The response, however, was negative, the sheriffs reporting that the mood in the country was hostile.

Consequently, when he returned to London in November, Richard's position had been weakened, the more so in that he lacked significant military force. Nevertheless, he immediately took the initiative, demanding that Gloucester, Arundel and Warwick come to meet him. They did not comply, but instead assembled their retinues at Harringay Park. When they did come to meet Richard on 17 November, they had sufficient force to overawe the king and guarantee their own safety. At this meeting they demanded the arrest pending trial in Parliament of five men: de la Pole, de Vere; Sir Nicholas Brembre; the Chief Justice of the King's Bench, Sir Robert Tresilian, who had given Richard a favourable constitutional opinion at Nottingham; and Alexander Neville, Archbishop of York, whom they considered a man unworthy of the office he held and to whom Richard had become close during the 1385 campaign in Scotland. Again, Richard was pushed onto the back foot, and he was forced to agree to a meeting of Parliament in February 1388.

Richard's only option, other than capitulation, was now the use of force. And this he opted for, sending de Vere to raise an army in Cheshire to suppress what was now clearly an armed rebellion. The move failed. On 19 December, as he marched south, de Vere was intercepted at Radcot Bridge in Oxfordshire by Henry of Bolingbroke, Gaunt's heir (since 1385 using one of his father's titles, Earl of Derby), who with the Earl of Nottingham had joined Gloucester and the other earls. The following day de Vere's force melted away and he fled to the coast and thence to the continent. The news of this scared Richard, prompting him to move into the Tower, where a few days later he was confronted by the rebellious earls.

They again threatened him with deposition, and it is possible that for a few days this almost happened. What saved Richard was the lack of agreement, or likelihood of an agreement, about a successor. Gloucester probably had designs on the throne, but there was no chance that the others would countenance that. Moreover, there was an heir presumptive in the person of Roger Mortimer, Fourth Earl of March, the grandson of Edward III's second son, Lionel, Duke of Clarence. A third factor was the Henry of Bolingbroke, Earl of Derby: if Gloucester had a claim to the throne as Edward III's fifth son, Gaunt, Edward III's third son, had a better one, and Bolingbroke was Gaunt's heir-apparent. With Gaunt away in Portugal and Castile, it fell to Bolingbroke to defend the Lancastrian interest, which almost certainly explains his late adherence to the rebellion.

Richard saved himself and his throne by agreeing to the arrest and trial before Parliament of fourteen named men. Five – de Vere, de la Pole, Nicholas Brembre, Sir Robert Tresilian, Chief Justice of the King's Bench and Alexander Neville, Archbishop of York – were 'appealed' (i.e. accused) of treason by the five earls; and nine others were 'impeached'. In effect, the earls, or 'the Appellants' as they were known as a result of their 'appeal', having learned of the legal weapon Richard had devised, seized the initiative and turned it against him.

The 'Merciless Parliament' sat for 122 days between 3 February 1388 and 4 June. In that time, the Appellants secured the conviction and execution of Sir Nicholas Brembre, Sir Robert Tresilian, and four Chamber Knights: Simon Burley, John Beauchamp, James Berners and John Salisbury. They also secured the conviction of Michael de la Pole, Robert de Vere and Alexander Neville, but not their execution, since they had fled abroad. The other judges who had advised Richard grovelled sufficiently to save their necks, although at the cost of banishment to Ireland. With the assistance of Pope Urban VI, who since the onset of the Great Schism had little option but to comply with the requests of the English government, Thomas Arundel was translated from Ely to York as Archbishop. This necessitated Alexander Neville's removal to another see. Urban's solution was to make him Bishop of St Andrews, a meaningless honour since that see was not vacant and was in Scotland, which owed allegiance to his rival.

Neville lived out the rest of his life, as did de Vere, in obscure and poverty stricken exile. Both men died in 1392.

The triumph of the Appellants was brief. Unlike most previous baronial rebels, they had no constitutional reform proposals: once they had got rid of the men they hated, they had nothing to offer but themselves. And what they had to offer proved inadequate, especially in the field of foreign affairs. As we have seen, Gaunt made a unilateral peace with Castile and Portugal, and declined to invade France from Gascony. Further north, Duke Jean IV paid homage to Charles VI of France for his Duchy of Brittany. And on the northern frontier, the Scots inflicted a serious defeat on an English army at Otterburn. It was not surprising, therefore, that the Commons in the Parliament that met at Cambridge in September had lost their previous enthusiasm for the Appellants. Their disillusionment hastened Richard's recovery of his authority. At a meeting of the royal council in May 1389, Richard announced that, as he was now of age (he was in fact twenty-two), he proposed to resume control of the government. There was no significant dissent.

What part did the Percy family play in this crisis? The brief answer is, very little. Sir Thomas Percy was abroad with Gaunt, at the forefront of his military and diplomatic activity in Spain and Portugal. His only contact with the Appellants was as Gaunt's emissary sent to inform them of the agreements Gaunt had made with the two Iberian kings. Similarly, Hotspur was absorbed with matters military, not political. In 1386, he spent some time at Calais and he was responsible for dispersing the French force besieging Brest; and, in 1388, he was active on the Border until his defeat and capture at Otterburn. There is no evidence of his being in any way involved with the political crisis. Given that his father was still alive and in England, it is unlikely that he would have had the scope for a political role.

In contrast, the Earl was involved, but only in a marginal way and seemingly not as a partisan. Although his concerns cannot be perceived with any certainty, they do seem to indicate a wish to play the role of conciliator, particularly in the last weeks of 1387 when the crisis appeared to be heading towards civil war. He may have tried to persuade the king that, despite their fears and deeply felt sense of injustice, his opponents were essentially loyal to him. Richard, on the other hand, may have tried to recruit the Earl to arrest the Earl of Arundel. When the 'Merciless Parliament' began its work, the Earl was present, but here too his stance was moderate. He was a member of the commission set up to investigate the activities of the Londoner, Nicholas Brembre, which reported that they could find nothing in his doings that made him worthy of death. Their conclusion did not save Brembre, who the Appellants were determined to execute. All in all, the Earl appears to have avoided involvement in a quarrel that did not directly concern him and in which northerners generally had only a passing interest.

FOUR

Counter-Revolution and Revolution, 1389–99

The political crisis of 1387–88 ended with 'a whimper not a bang'. There was no serious resistance to Richard's resumption of the direction of government, largely because the regime of the Duke of Gloucester and the Earls of Arundel and Warwick had failed to maintain widespread support. From this time until the summer of 1399, the political life of the country centred on the king, and without significant opposition. In part, this was due to Richard's circumspect approach, evident in his apparent willingness to work with the Council and his noted failure to insist on the recall of his erstwhile favourite, Robert de Vere; but also, perhaps, because of the natural inclination of the political nation to see a return to the normal governmental process in which the monarch played the leading role.

In the years that followed, two facets of the king's character became more apparent. One was that, unlike his father and paternal grandfather, he was a man of peace, not interested in war or being a warrior. Although he delighted in the pageantry of heraldry and chivalry, including presiding at tournaments, and led two expeditions to Ireland, and one to Scotland, he showed no inclination or eagerness to take part in combat, mock or real. Want of enthusiasm for matters military was always a minus mark for a medieval monarch and a peace policy towards France was bound to be opposed in some quarters.

The other aspect was his concept of royal status. He required to be known as 'prince' and to be addressed not as 'my lord' but as 'your highness' or 'your majesty', terms that carried the clear overtones of absolute sovereignty. For the same reason, he placed great emphasis on ceremonial forms and rituals that emphasised his unique status and condition as king. Both Richard Jones and Nigel Saul have argued that he had been made aware of, and influenced by, the teachings of theorists of monarchical power and authority, particularly those of the late thirteenth-century writer, Giles of Rome, a copy of whose *De Regimine Principum* is known to have belonged to his tutor, Sir Simon Burley. At the heart of their argument is the notion that the prince was the sole constitutional authority and the sole source of law and that the Roman law dictum 'the prince's will has the force of law' did and should obtain. That Richard was an apt pupil is amply revealed in his best-remembered remark that 'the laws of England were in his mouth'. These ideas, however, were not adopted and expressed simply for their own sake. Their purpose was to justify Richard's moves to increase his power as king and enforce obedience on his subjects. In all of this, Richard was at one with his fellow European monarchs, who were attempting to elevate their status and to recover political powers lost to their subjects in the early decades of the century through the rise of representitive institutions.

What was hidden at this stage, and which did not become apparent until the later years of the decade, was his deeply vengeful nature. It is hard to believe that there was not a direct link between this and the political beliefs with which he was brought up and which he adopted with such conviction. Added to this were his previous experiences. The perilous confrontation with Wat Tyler and the rebel mob in 1381, when he was only fourteen years old and in which he displayed cool courage, was an unnerving experience, the effect of which may never have fully left him. On top of this was the trauma of the more recent crisis in which he came very close to losing his throne through the actions of men, including his own uncle, who should have been his natural associates. These experiences must have bred in him a permanent sense of personal insecurity and a deep mistrust and fear of those who opposed him. However, if in the early 1390s he was already resolved upon revenge, he dissembled very effectively. He had learned to play the political game.

The New Regime

In these years, he had two main policies. One was to achieve a permanent and comprehensive peace with England's principal enemies, France and Scotland. Apart from his own natural inclination, Richard appears to have recognised that the war with France was failing to achieve its aims while costing a great deal of money, most of which derived from taxation. Generally, the Commons, the source of taxation, was willing to oblige if their investment brought success, but turned critical when the war went badly. In this policy he had the support of Gaunt, whom he made Duke of Aquitaine in March 1390. The French government also was strongly inclined to peace. Charles VI, who came of age in 1389, was non-belligerent and in this he had the backing of his uncle, the Duke of Burgundy, whose Flemish towns were dependent upon trade with England. Similarly, the new king of Scotland, Robert III, was old and politically weak. In all three countries, however, there were those who were opposed to the ending of the war. In England, the old Appellants, Gloucester and Arundel, argued against peace, and they did have the support of some members of the gentry, for whom peace would dash their prospects of booty and ransoms. Likewise, in France the king's brother, Louis, Duke of Orleans, was disinclined to peace; and in Scotland, the Earls of Douglas and March could see gains to be made through continuing hostilities.

Permanent peace proved elusive, however. With France the problem was, as it had been since the thirteenth century, the status of the King of England as Duke of Aquitaine. The French might be willing to be generous in the matter of the extent of the duchy, but what they were not prepared to concede was a relationship less than that of liege homage. This was a concession no king of England could make: it would be a betrayal of his inheritance; and it would provoke outrage among important sections of his subjects. In the end, the best that could be achieved was a twenty-eight-year truce. This was agreed in 1396 and was sealed by the marriage of Richard to Charles VI's daughter, Isabelle (Richard had been a widower since the death in 1394 of his first wife, Anne, daughter of the Holy Roman Emperor, Charles IV). The fact that Isabelle was only eight years old (and not a mature young woman, as portrayed by Shakespeare in *Richard II*) was to have political ramifications in England three years later. The relationship with Scotland took a similar course. With France out of the game, Scotland could not risk war with England, but the terms that England proposed, including homage by the Scottish king and the cession of territory, were unacceptable. As a result, no peace treaty was agreed and the absence of war was maintained by a series of truces.

Richard's other problem was Ireland, where the area under English authority had been shrinking since the 1320s and the Gaelic chiefs, notably Art MacMurrough, the self-styled King of Leinster, were beyond control. One serious consequence of this was that Ireland, instead of being profitable, had become a financial liability. In late 1394, therefore, Richard led an impressive expedition to Ireland, where he stayed until the following spring. Thomas Percy played an important part in this enterprise. By now Steward of the Household (see below), he commanded a contingent of troops; and as Admiral with his own ship, the *Trinite*, he was responsible for getting Richard's force across the Irish Sea. The gains from the expedition, although impressive, were superficial. Sufficient force was applied to secure the formal submission of the Irish leaders, but their real power had not been seriously undermined, let alone destroyed. The nineteen-year-old Roger Mortimer, Earl of March, who possessed extensive lands (or claims to lands) in Ireland as Earl of Ulster, was left to continue the policy as King's Lieutenant, as best he could.

The other policy pursued by Richard was the creation of a court faction, a group of men closely bound to him and upon whose support and loyalty he could rely. Its most prominent members, drawn from the nobility, were elevated in status by Richard in 1390. They were: his older half-brother, Thomas Holand, whom he made Earl of Kent (and who was succeeded by his son, also Thomas, in 1397); his younger half-brother, John Holand, whom he made Earl of Huntingdon; his nephew Edward, son of Edmund of Langley, Duke of York, whom he made Earl of Rutland; John Beaufort, the oldest of Gaunt's sons by his third wife, Katherine Swynford, whom he made Earl of Somerset; John Montague, Earl of Salisbury and Thomas, Lord Despenser. To this group was added Thomas Mowbray, Earl of Nottingham, who, although one of the Appellants, was restored to royal favour. He also built up a following of knights, most notably Sir William Scrope (or Lescrope), who was perhaps closer to him than any other man, Sir John Bussy (or Bushy), Sir William Bagot, Sir Henry Green, Sir Richard Stury (or Sturry) and Sir Lewis Clifford. Over and above this group he took steps to create his own affinity: by the later years of the decade 80 knights and 125 esquires had entered his service. It was an impressive performance, but it was flawed in that it was essentially divisive, not inclusive: those who were 'not one of us' were bound to feel excluded and perhaps threatened.

How did the Percys accommodate to this new regime? Basically, the answer is that Sir Thomas Percy, although of an older generation, became an active and influential insider at the centre, a man close to the king, while his brother and his nephew, particularly the latter, were more neutral and distant, men of the periphery. Now in his mid-forties, Thomas Percy may have decided that service abroad was no longer attractive, particularly as Richard's 'peace policy' and Gaunt's decision to renounce his claim to the throne of Castile meant that France and Spain had ceased to offer much prospect of profit. For his part, Richard would have remembered Percy's service during the critical days of 1381 and would have recognised that a man of Percy's intelligence, ability and experience at a high level in diplomatic, administrative and military and naval matters would make him a worthwhile recruit to his coterie. Moreover, being in France and Spain during the crisis of 1386–88 meant that Percy did not become politically tainted by association with the Appellants. Had he been in England, there was a risk that he would have been drawn into opposition by the Duke of Gloucester, with whom, as Earl of Buckingham, he was closely associated in the early 1380s. These mutual considerations help to explain Percy's appointment in 1390 as Chamberlain of the Household. In accepting the appointment, he ended his service with John of Gaunt, who was made Duke of Gascony in the same year. Three years later, Percy's status within the royal circle was confirmed by his appointment as Steward of the Household, a post he was to retain for the rest of the reign.

The office of Steward was, together with that of the Chamberlain (who supervised the king's private apartment and, more importantly, controlled access to the king's person), the most important and powerful in the Household. Its holder was responsible for order and discipline and the efficient running of an organisation that comprised, depending on whether a state of peace or of war existed, between 400 and 700 persons. Since it rarely stayed more than two months in any of the royal residences, logistic ability was essential in the role. Distance moved on any occasion was normally not great, since, like his predecessor, for most of his reign Richard's favoured residences were close to London, principally Eltham and Sheen, on which he spent considerably in the 1380s. It was at Sheen that his first wife, Anne, died in the summer of 1394, and in the following April, in a theatrical gesture of grief, he ordered that it be rased to the ground. In its place, he developed the hunting lodge known as Windsor Manor, in the Great Park five miles from the castle. He also made some use of the palace at Kings Langley (Hertfordshire), but none of the royal manors at Havering (Essex), Leeds Castle (Kent) and Woodstock (Oxfordshire). However, after 1396, almost certainly for tactical reasons, Richard and his court forsook this restricted radius and spent much time in the Midlands, Lichfield and Nottingham seemingly becoming the king's favourite places of residence.

In carrying out his duties, the Steward had to work closely with the Keeper of the Wardrobe, the chief financial officer of the Household, in supervising the inflow of money and expenditure on goods, services and fees. The Steward also needed to have had military experience in that the Household included king's knights and esquires in residence and his bodyguard of thirty sergeants at arms.

Because of his closeness to the king, the Steward was used in many other roles. Percy's military service in Ireland in 1394 and 1395 has been already noted. In civil affairs, he was usually a member of Parliament, and his standing with the king made him a significant member of any diplomatic mission: Percy, for example, was on those headed by Gaunt in 1392 and 1393 that attempted to negotiate a permanent peace with France. Until her death in 1394, he was also a member of the council that supervised the queen's affairs. And in 1395 one of his easier duties was to present to the king, Jean Froissart, the great publicist for the European chivalric ideals and activities, who came to England to give Richard his book, *Livre d'Amours*.

Nor were his duties confined to court and occasional forays abroad. Like others with the king's confidence, he was given important roles in provincial administration. In 1390, he was appointed Justice of South Wales, Keeper of Newcastle Emlyn and its lordship in Carmarthenshire, and Keeper of Haverford Castle and its lordship in Pembrokeshire. Although these offices carried great responsibility and yielded considerable income, the routine work could be done by deputies. Together these posts made Thomas Percy the most powerful royal official in South Wales. His income was also increased by the grant of the customs duties on wines coming into Milford and advantageous leases of estates that were temporarily in the Crown's hand as the result of minorities. Then, in 1398, he was made Captain of Calais following the dismissal of Thomas Mowbray, Earl of Nottingham (see below). There is no doubt that throughout the decade Thomas Percy was a highly regarded, most useful and consequently well-rewarded member of the royal household.

Percy was also involved in a *cause célèbre* that reached its final stage at the beginning of the 1390s. This was the long-running case in the Court of Chivalry (which incidentally reveals the huge importance the amigerous classes attached to symbols of honour) between a Cheshire knight, Sir Robert Grosvenor, and a Yorkshire knight, Sir Richard Scrope, who was to become First Lord Scrope of Bolton. The issue between them was the right to use the armorial device *azure a bend or* (a blue ground with a broad diagonal gold band running from the top right corner of the shield). The case began during the 1385 invasion of Scotland, when Grosvenor challenged Scrope's right to the use of the arms. The Duke of Gloucester, the Constable and thereby *ex officio* head of the Court of Chivalry, commissioned five knights to tour the country and take depositions from as many men as possible in an effort to establish the truth of the matter. They interviewed no fewer than 466 knights and esquires, including the poet, Geoffrey Chaucer, and listed churches where the disputed arms were displayed. Thomas Percy was among those who made depositions, in his case on 16 June 1386 in the Carmelite friary at Plymouth, where he was waiting to embark with Gaunt for Castile. Later in the year, on 30 October, Hotspur made his deposition to Sir John Derwentwater, one of the five commissioners, in the refectory of Westminster Abbey.

The political upheaval during the years 1386–88 meant that the case was not brought to its conclusion until the spring of 1389. Although the verdict was given in Scrope's favour, Grosvenor's cause had sufficient strength for him to be offered a modified version of the arms: *azure a bend or, bordure argent,* that is, the arms with a silver border. This addition would have made it a mark of **cadency**, which Grosvenor's pride would not allow him to accept; consequently, he appealed against the verdict. Percy headed the committee that reconsidered the matter, but in May 1390, they confirmed the original decision. Costs of £466 13s 4d (£466.67) were awarded against Grosvenor, with an additional 50 marks (£33.34) amercement. He was excused the latter, however, at the request of his opponent.

As Steward, Thomas Percy was an important and influential member of the royal court, although he was probably not among Richard's closest familiars. The Earl, however, was clearly not a member of king's inner circle. But, as a wealthy, powerful and able member of the nobility, he was of considerable political importance, a fact underlined by his membership of, and frequent attendance at, the Council. In 1389, for example, he persuaded the Council not to immediately recognise Boniface IX, elected pope on the death of Urban VI, in order to give the government greater leverage in the matter of papal provisions. But his main interest was almost certainly the northern Border, where, it is fair to assume, he wished to re-establish and as far as possible make permanent Percy dominance. The situation there had been disturbed by Hotspur's defeat and consequent captivity in Scotland in the summer and autumn of 1388. In his place as Warden of the East March, the Appellants appointed John Stanley, whom Richard replaced in June 1389 by Thomas Mowbray, Earl of Nottingham. Although Hotspur was given the less prestigious West March in June 1390, the East March, where the more important Percy interests were located, was in the hands of a powerful outsider. The Earl had to be compensated, however, and he was given a post of equal if not greater prestige, that of Captain of Calais.

Calais, which had developed from a fishing village into an important port in the thirteenth and early fourteenth centuries, fell to Edward III's army in August 1347 after a year-long siege. Most of its inhabitants were expelled and replaced by English settlers: Edward's intention was to make Calais an English colony. English control was not confined to the town, but extended beyond it to include the Lordship of Marck, with its two important castles at Marck and Oye. These, together with the castle in the town and the fort that dominated its harbour entrance, made Calais a military enclave of some strength. And it became stronger in the years immediately following as English forces captured six more neighbouring castles at Coulogne, Sangatte, Guines, Frethun, Hammes and Poyle.

The colony reached its greatest extent as a result of the Treaty of Bretigny in 1360, when three-quarters of the neighbouring County of Guines was acquired, that is, the lordships of Guines, Ardres and Audruicq, but not that of Tournehem. However, among the many English losses in the period of renewed warfare after 1369 were most of these recent acquisitions: in 1377 the French recovered control of Ardres and Audruicq, leaving England with only Guines. Nevertheless, the town of Calais, together with the lordships of Marck and Guines, formed a substantial enclave, with a coastal stretch of twenty miles, a landward depth of ten miles and an area of 120 square miles. And its importance was not solely military and strategic: in 1363 the Staple, the commercial monopoly through which almost all of England's wool was exported and from which the English Crown derived a substantial income, was transferred to Calais.

The Captain of Calais controlled the appointment of the commanders of all the castles, the combined garrisons of which totalled around 800 men in time of peace. This force was the closest the medieval English state came to having a standing army. Moreover, its annual peacetime cost of about £10,000 was one of the largest items in the Crown's budget. Consequently, he who occupied the post had considerable power at his disposal and, from the Crown's standpoint, he needed to be someone in whom complete trust could be placed. Therefore, appointing a southerner as Warden of the East March and a northerner as Captain of Calais may have been a deliberate move to take powerful men out of their natural political habitats and, by doing so, to weaken them. If so, it was a short-lived experiment. In the summer of 1391, the Earl persuaded the king to allow him to exchange roles with Thomas Mowbray, who probably preferred Calais to the Border. The fact that the Earl was eager to give up such a lucrative and politically powerful post testifies to the importance he attached to restoring complete Percy control in the Border zone.

With a truce in place, even though there were minor infractions, Hotspur was not fully occupied as Warden of the West March, many of whose duties could be discharged by locally based deputies. Consequently, it is not surprising to find him elsewhere. In the spring of 1390, typically, he was involved in one of the more renowned of the international tournaments of the fourteenth century, that at St Inglevert, a village just beyond the boundary of the Calais Pale. It was the brainchild of a group of French knights, the most famous of whom was the 24-year-old Jean de Boucicaut, who was to become Marshal of France, to be taken prisoner at Agincourt in 1415 and to die a captive in Yorkshire in 1421. Boucicaut had already seen serious action in Flanders and Acquitaine and also, more frivolously, in the Holy Land and in Egypt, where he was taken prisoner and had to be ransomed. He was, to his contemporaries, the glamorous embodiment of adventurous chivalry.

The form of the tournament, as devised by him and his associates, was to occupy a field at St Inglevert, and then challenge the knights of Europe to remove them. In part, this was an antidote to the boredom arising from the military inactivity following the truce between England and France, but it was also provoked by the bragging of English knights who, with the end of hostilities, appear to have been visiting France as tourists. The challenge was widely advertised and it attracted a large number of knights from as far away as Bohemia and Germany, as well as about 100 from England. Although Froissart's blow-by-blow account of the event may not be entirely accurate, he is probably correct in his description of knights challenging one of the 'home team' by touching the shield (which hung outside his tent for this purpose) of the one he wished to fight. Each contest took the form of a joust of three passes, none of which appears to have caused more damage than cuts, bruises and hurt pride. Nor, it seems, was it an entirely male occasion, since there were rest days when it became a pleasant social occasion, when the knights were joined by their ladies. Hotspur, newly ransomed from captivity in Scotland, took part in this affair as a member of the team assembled by Gaunt's heir, Henry of Bolingbroke, Earl of Derby. The French knights considered Hotspur and his colleagues to be the most courageous of all their opponents.

There is no evidence, however, that Hotspur took part in the Smithfield tournament in October of the same year. This event was by way of being a 'return match' for tournaments held in Paris the previous year. It was organised by Richard II and was very much a royal occasion: only twenty knights took part, all Knights of the Garter and personally very close to Richard. It was at this event that Richard first distributed what became his famous badge, the white hart. Sheila Lindenbaum has suggested that this tournament had a definite political purpose in proclaiming a new start to his reign after the trauma of the Appellant crisis.

Two years later, Hotspur was engaged in more serious business, this time in the company of Bolingbroke's father. The scene was again France, but this time Aquitaine, not Artois. In March 1390, Richard granted Gaunt the Duchy of Gascony for life to hold of him, Richard, as King of France. By this move he hoped to solve the problem of what to do with Gaunt, who had recently given up his title as King of Castile and Leon, and to put the Gascon problem at one remove from his own person. If it seemed neat to Richard and desirable to Gaunt, it horrified the Gascon nobility and the *jurats* (ruling magistrates) of Bordeaux. By doing what he did, Richard broke the undertaking given by his ancestors that Gascony would never be separated from the English Crown. The most the Gascons would willingly accept was the dukedom in the hands of the heir to the throne, as had happened in the case of the Black Prince. Behind this was the genuine fear that this endangered the privileges they had been granted by English kings.

Hotspur was introduced into this difficult and turbulent situation in 1393, when he took up the post of Gaunt's lieutenant in succession to Sir William Scrope. On arrival at Bordeaux, he was admitted to the town, but as the king's lieutenant, not Gaunt's. He had to hold the fort until late in the following year, when Gaunt arrived with an army of 1,500 men. This, and emollient assurances given by Richard to a Gascon deputation, were sufficient to get the arrangement accepted. Even so, Gaunt had to tread carefully, overturning one of Hotspur's decisions, which had offended the *jurats* of Bordeaux. Gaunt stayed in Gascony only for a few months, when he exercised his ducal authority in person. Thereafter, although details are missing, it is probable that Hotspur remained in office until he was succeeded by Gaunt's son, John Beaufort, in 1397.

When at home, Hotspur was by no means idle. Evidence in the Fine Rolls shows him to have been an operator in the short-term property market. In 1391, he acquired the keeping of a manor forfeited by John de Ask, and in 1393 the marriage and lands during his minority of Robert de Stodham. Both were Yorkshire esquires. In the latter year, he was granted the keepership of part of Inglewood Forest in Cumberland and, after his return from Gascony, he leased royal property near Clitheroe and two vacant plots in Berwick upon Tweed, where he undertook to rebuild two derelict windmills. For these properties he was required to pay annual rents totalling just under £25. It is safe to assume that he would have calculated on making a considerably greater sum.

These multifarious activities at home and abroad did not mean that Hotspur was entirely absent from court. He is known to have spent part of the summer of 1393, together with his uncle, as a member of the royal party hunting in the New Forest. This was not without its penalties, however: on 22 August the royal party dined at Titchfield Abbey, Hotspur footing the bill. Overall, however, it is clear that Hotspur was not a natural courtier.

Richard's Revenge

In the light of what happened between July 1397 and February 1398, it is arguable that behind Richard's policies and actions since 1389 lay a conscious and carefully considered intention of completing his 'counter-revolution'. This had two aims. The first was to avenge the humiliation he suffered in 1387 and 1388 by destroying those responsible for it. This may be seen as the negative aim. More positively, he intended to use the destruction of his enemies as the means of advancing and increasing his power as king, so that the reality of his position would correspond to his conception of it. Why he made his move when he did is still, and may remain, a matter of speculation, but it may be that he was now free of any counsel of caution close to him. His new wife, Isabelle, was a child, and although Queen Anne is not known to have been a politically influential figure, Richard's strong attachment to her argues that she may have exercised a moderating influence over him. Alternatively, he may have feared or believed (and here the evidence is ambiguous) that his old opponents, and Gloucester in particular, were plotting to move against him again: this time he would not show his hand until after he had made the decisive move.

Whatever the reason, Richard made his move on 10 July at a banquet at Cold Harbour, the Earl of Huntingdon's London house near St Paul's.

The three invited guests were the Earls of Warwick and Arundel and his uncle, the Duke of Gloucester. Only Warwick accepted. At the end of what was an apparently convivial meal, the mood suddenly changed and Warwick was arrested and hustled off to the Tower. Richard then personally led a mounted troop to Pleshey in Essex to arrest the unsuspecting Gloucester, who was placed in the custody of the Earl of Kent and subsequently transferred to secure custody at Calais. Here it is worth noting that it is likely that, as Steward of the Household, Thomas Percy was present at the Cold Harbour feast and in the group that rode out to Pleshey. If so, he would have been fully apprised of Richard's intentions. Arundel, who was uneasy, also did not attend, but remained in his castle at Reigate until he was persuaded to give himself up by his brother, Thomas, Archbishop of Canterbury, who himself was deceived as to Richard's intent. This became clear four weeks later when, in a carefully stagemanaged performance at Nottingham Castle, the three men were formally 'appealed' of treason by the Earls of Rutland, Kent, Huntingdon, Somerset, Nottingham and Salisbury. It was a deliberately ironic and bitter reversal of the action the accused had taken against the courtiers of Richard's youth.

The resolution took place in the Parliament that met at Westminster between 17 and 30 September. Proceedings opened with the traditional sermon, preached by Edmund Stafford, Bishop of Exeter, who took as his text the ominous words *One king shall be king unto them all* (Ezekiel 37: 22). The following day, the pardons issued after the crisis of 1386–88 were revoked, and treason was given a much looser and broader definition. The stage was now set for a series of show trials.

It began on 21 September, with Gaunt presiding in his capacity as Steward of England. The first of the accused was Arundel, who denied treason and put up a characteristically robust and defiant defence. This, however, served only to ensure conviction and a one-way journey to Tower Hill and the executioner's sword. Three days later it should have been Gloucester's turn, but it was reported that he had died at Calais. Rumours of his death had been circulating for some time, and because of its obvious convenience, foul play was suspected. And rightly, since, although there is no conclusive proof, it is all but certain that Gloucester was murdered on Richard's orders and that the man immediately responsible was the Captain of Calais, Thomas Mowbray, Earl of Nottingham. Nevertheless, and this time with Thomas Percy in the chair, a confession of treason allegedly made by Gloucester before he died was read out and as a result he was posthumously condemned as a traitor. On the same day, but in private, Archbishop Arundel was deprived of his temporalities and sent into exile, Richard mendaciously assuring him that his sojourn abroad would be brief and that he would not be deprived of his office. Then on the 28th Warwick was brought before Parliament. Unlike Arundel, he confessed, grovelled and begged for mercy. Surprisingly, perhaps, he got it: his punishment was confiscation of his estates and exile for life to the Isle of Man.

Richard celebrated the successful conclusion of his revenge-taking by announcing 'promotions' for ten of his supporters. His half-brother, John Holand, Earl of Huntingdon, became Duke of Exeter and his nephew, Thomas Holand, Earl of Kent, became Duke of Surrey; Edward, Earl of Rutland became Duke of Aumerle; Thomas Mowbray, Earl of Nottingham became Duke of Norfolk; Gaunt's eldest son, Henry of Bolingbroke, Earl of Derby became Duke of Hereford; John Beaufort, Earl of Somerset became Marquis of Dorset; Ralph, Lord Neville became Earl of Westmorland; Thomas, Lord Despenser became Earl of Gloucester; Sir William Scrope became Earl of Wiltshire. And Thomas Percy became Earl of Worcester, joining his brother in the ranks of the nobility.

His reward was not merely honorary. To maintain his new status as earl, he was granted an annual income of 700 marks (£466.67). Richard's ability to honour this grant was made possible by his possession of the estates of the three recently executed traitors, which he distributed among his leading supporters. Percy's share comprised nineteen manors and lordships in Shropshire formerly belonging to the fallen Earl of Arundel and four manors in Essex, Norfolk and Kent that had belonged to the Duke of Gloucester, as well as the reversion of three manors currently held of Gloucester's estate by Maud, Countess of Oxford. Together with the income from the manors with which his father had invested him, his income from land was now substantial. Much more, however, came from fees and annuities. By 1400, in addition to Edward III's pension, he was in receipt of over £400 from the castle and county of Pembroke and the South Wales exchequer, over £100 from London, over £300 from the manor of Eye in Suffolk and nearly £200 from the Exchequer. His potential annual income was therefore at least £1,500, although it is safe to assume that he would not have received all elements in full. Nevertheless, service at the court and in the cause of Richard II had paid Thomas Percy handsomely in status and income.

The reward underlines the extent to which Thomas Percy had assisted Richard in his act of vengeance. Not only did he act as president of the court on the occasion of the posthumous trial of the king's uncle, but he was also chosen to act as proctor for the clerical members of Parliament. They had attempted to avoid any involvement by protesting that their holy orders precluded their participation in legal proceedings that could end in execution; but their protest was overruled. Having Percy as their proctor was a fig leaf, but it was the best cover they could get. In this capacity, he voted for the guilt of the accused, and at the high mass in Westminster Abbey to mark the end of the session, he took the oath on their behalf to uphold in perpetuity all that had been done in that parliamentary session.

How genuine his enthusiasm was cannot be known. He may have been fully with Richard and in total support of his aspirations and actions. On the other hand, he may have been the cynical opportunist or cool realist, who recognised that backing Richard was the way to wealth and status while opposing him could lead to the block. In any case, as head of the royal household he had little option but to go along, and with a show of enthusiasm, with Richard's scheme; to have declined or demurred would have been suicidal. His prominent role was in conspicuous contrast to that played by his elder brother. The Earl's only apparent involvement was as a member of the commission of five noblemen headed by Gaunt, which Richard sent to examine Arundel's corpse and then to rebury it in an unmarked grave, the aim being to prevent the growth of a cult, something that the king must have feared.

Four days before the promotions were announced, Richard began the process of increasing his power and his grip upon the country. On the 25th, he raised the earldom of Chester, long vested in the Crown, to the status of Principality, and expanded its geographical size by including the tri-partite county of Flint and attaching to it three former Arundel properties: the lordships of Bromyard and Yale, Chirk and Shrawardine, and Oswestry. The Principality was to have its own government staffed by Richard's supporters and to be virtually a state within a state. Throughout his reign, Richard had been very attached to Cheshire and it was now evident that he intended to make it a fortress and his power base. This was further underlined by his moves to create a Cheshire army. He raised a permanent force of 750, including 10 knights, 97 esquires and 311 archers and he ordered that no one was to recruit archers in the Principality until 2,300 had been attached to the king's retinue. This, combined with his expanded affinity, he hoped would provide him with the military force that he had fatally lacked in 1387.

On 30 September, Parliament was prorogued until January 1398, when it reconvened at Shrewsbury. During the interval a development occurred about which there is still uncertainty and which, unlike many of the events of the recent past, was unplanned. It began in December 1397 as two of the newly promoted nobles, Henry of Bolingbroke, now Duke of Hereford, and Thomas Mowbray, now Duke of Norfolk, were riding from Brentford to London. In the course of their conversation, it would seem that Mowbray told Bolingbroke that they were not safe and that the king intended to destroy them for their parts in the Radcot Bridge affair eleven years before. Furthermore, he claimed that the men closest to Richard, namely the Duke of Surrey and the Earls of Wiltshire, Salisbury and Gloucester, had planned to assassinate the two of them and Bolingbroke's father, Gaunt, after the first session of Parliament, but that he, together with the Dukes of Aumerle and Exeter and Thomas Percy, Earl of Worcester, had managed to prevent this happening.

There may have been some truth in this, since it is clear that the huge estates of the Lancaster family excited a great deal of envy, and for Richard to have the disposal of them would add greatly to his resources and scope for patronage. Moreover, since Richard had no heir of his body (and his marriage to a child suggested that begetting one was not of paramount importance to him), Gaunt, or far more likely Bolingbroke, would probably succeed him, especially as the Earl of March was occupied in Ireland and the Duke of Gloucester was dead. If true, it would suggest that there were divisions at court and that Thomas Percy, while prepared to accept the liquidation of the past, may not have been willing to be party to a violent reordering of the future.

To Mowbray's consternation, Bolingbroke recounted the story to his father, who related it to the king. In fear, Mowbray absented himself from the new session of Parliament, where Bolingbroke was free to present a version of the story, to his credit and Mowbray's detriment. Bolingbroke may have been driven by fear, but his move certainly can be construed as opportunism. The result was that Mowbray was removed from his offices. Before this episode reached its conclusion, however, the second session of Parliament accomplished a great deal towards the advancement of Richard's programme. All the acts of the 'Merciless Parliament' were rescinded and a pliant Commons voted the king duties on the export of wool and leather for life and three and a half subsidies, thus helping to ensure that their services would not be needed for several years. Moreover, they delegated their power to deal with outstanding petitions to a standing committee of six knights and eighteen lords, one of whom was the Earl of Northumberland.

In the months that followed the closure of Parliament, Richard tightened his grip on local government. He set about ensuring that the crucial officers of the shire, the sheriffs and the justices of the peace, were as far as possible men of his choosing or known supporters. He also increased his financial solvency by the time-honoured method of the forced loan. In addition, he obliged sixteen counties in the south-east to elect proctors, who were required to sign charters on behalf of their counties acknowledging their collective complicity in the Radcot Bridge campaign and placing their lives and property at his disposal. In effect, he required these counties, as a means of obtaining pardons for their 'offence', to create swords of Damocles, which he then hung over their heads. These 'blank charters', as they were known, together with the undisciplined behaviour of his Cheshire archers, who at times acted like hired thugs, added to the violent elimination of his old enemies, aroused fear and a sense of unease in the country. He must have increasingly appeared to many as a king intent on terrorising his subjects into obedience, rather than providing them with good government. The word 'tyranny', so often applied to his rule in the late 1390s, does not seem misused.

The same months also saw the resolution of the Bolingbroke–Mowbray affair. On 23 February the two dukes appeared before the king at Oswestry, where Mowbray denied everything, but was nonetheless placed in custody. A month later, on 19 March, the parliamentary standing committee, of which the Earl was a member, at a meeting at Bristol, concluded that the evidence was inadequate and therefore the matter should be decided by judicial combat. The matter was again aired at a meeting of the King's Council at Windsor on 28 April, where Bolingbroke, presumably in the belief that attack is the best form of defence, expanded his list of accusations against Mowbray to include the murder of Gloucester. This for sure was not a matter that Richard dared allow to be aired in public, with the result that the decision to put the issue into the hands of the Court of Chivalry was confirmed, the trial by battle to take place at Coventry on 16 September. In itself this was, according to the ideas of the time, an acceptable means of resolution. What gave cause for concern was that the Court of Chivalry was given authority to deal with all cases where the 'fame and condition of the king's person' were impugned: very wide powers and a very loose definition.

As Anthony Tuck remarked, the combat at Coventry bade fair to be 'the social event of the year'. Indeed, a great crowd assembled at the lists, where the two men, both of whom had sent abroad for the best possible arms and armour, were on the point of commencing their fight to the death, when Richard intervened to stop the contest, doubtless to the chagrin of the spectators. This he was fully entitled to do under martial law. Instead of allowing this primitive means of judgement to take its course, he imposed his own arbitration. Mowbray was banished for life and Bolingbroke for ten years (reduced to six on the eve of his departure), with the proviso that he could appoint proctors to administer the Lancastrian estates, should his father die during his absence, an event that was almost certain to occur. This decision probably reflects fairly accurately the degrees of 'guilt' of the two men; but almost certainly other, political, considerations were of overriding importance. By his action, Richard asserted his control of the situation and obviated the potentially dangerous situation of the winner remaining in England, free to peddle his version of events.

The part played by Sir Thomas Percy in Richard's revenge was important and is clear enough, even though his beliefs and motives cannot be fathomed, and it earned him substantial social and economic advancement. In contrast, his brother the Earl was adversely affected by royal policy. In fact, Richard's move to tighten his control over his realm can be said to have begun two years before his action against the old Appellants with what proved to be a series of moves guaranteed to undermine the Percy position in the Border zone. In June 1395, Hotspur was removed from the wardenship of the West March and the post given to a southerner, John, Lord Beaumont. Then a year later, in June 1396, the Earl was removed as Warden of the East March, although Hotspur was his replacement. But the Percys continued to be excluded from the West March. Following Beaumont's death, the office was granted, firstly in 1396 to the king's half-brother, John Holand, Earl of Huntingdon (who became Duke of Exeter the following year), and then in 1398 to Richard's cousin, Edward, Duke of Aumerle, both members of the king's innermost circle. Moreover, Aumerle was granted the wardship and marriage of the underage Thomas Umfraville, whose Lordship of Redesdale lay within the East March.

But, for the Percys, worse was to follow. In the same year, Richard reintroduced the novel arrangement of the early 1380s by again placing Gaunt in overriding command on the Border as Lieutenant in the Marches, with authority over all officials. These included new offices, the Keepers of the Truce, to which were appointed the Dukes of Aumerle and Exeter for respectively the West and East Marches. In addition, Richard appointed four of his most trusted supporters, including Sir John Bushy and Sir Henry Greene, to deal with violators of the truce.

Richard's prime purpose in these moves was to ensure that the truce with Scotland remained undisturbed. Gaunt, as a member of the royal family, would have the standing to deal with the Scots at the highest level, and the presence of southerners would, hopefully, keep the warlike inclinations of the men of the Border in check. Richard and his circle may have had considerable doubts about the commitment of the Earl and Hotspur to the truce. But it is equally likely that these moves were intended to impose a greater degree of royal authority in the far north. If so, Richard was confronting the Earl in the area he regarded as his own back yard. However, at this stage Richard was moving cautiously and astutely. The fact that he retained Hotspur as Warden of the East March shows either that he feared to eradicate Percy power entirely, or that he recognised that peace in the Border zone required their positive co-operation.

As part of this policy of containment was his advancement of Ralph, Lord Neville of Raby, an exact contemporary of Hotspur, who became Lord of Raby on the death of his father in 1388. In the following nine years, Neville gained wide experience of war and administration in the north. Having proved his worth, in 1397 he was created Earl of Westmorland and to support this status he was granted the large manors of Penrith and Sowerby in Cumberland and the lease of the castle of Appleby in Westmorland. These grants made him a powerful figure in the West March and an obvious counterweight to the Earl. Two years earlier he had been granted a twelve-year lease of the Honour of Richmond, with its important castles at Richmond and Bowes, which added to his status in the North Riding of Yorkshire. But the Nevilles were not solely reliant on royal favours. In 1376, Ralph's father, John, had acquired the Northumberland barony of Bywell as a result of the reversion granted to them forty years earlier by Mary of St Pol, Countess of Pembroke. Then in 1397 Ralph secured the neighbouring barony of Bolbec, this time as the result of a reversion made in 1379 by Sir Ralph Hastings. These acquisitions gave the Nevilles a significant foothold in Northumberland. By 1397, therefore, Ralph Neville had achieved a degree of parity with the Percys in all three northern counties. Six years later, his enhanced power in the north was to be of crucial political importance.

The Earl would have recognised that while Richard was on the throne there was no way he could be certain of acquiring and retaining the permanent monopoly of Border offices and a free hand in Border affairs. Could he have done better by attempting to ingratiate himself with the king? He was not excluded from national politics, as his membership of the Council and his occasional appearance centre stage demonstrate; but he seems never to have made any move to become part of the king's inner circle. And nor does Hotspur, who may even have spent some time in the 1390s practising his trade as a soldier on crusade. And the Earl appears in no way to have gained from having his only brother as an important member of the royal court. At this stage the two men appear to have been following parallel but separate paths, although Thomas Percy was not among those closest to the king, and those who were, were either of Richard's generation or linked to him in blood.

Meanwhile, Richard also moved to secure a greater hold on Ireland. On 27 July, he appointed the Duke of Surrey (who, it was rumoured, was to be made King of Ireland) as Lieutenant in Ireland in place of Roger Mortimer, Earl of March. Richard may well have been planning to go further and destroy Mortimer so as to obtain his huge estates in Wales and Ireland, which he would then distribute among his supporters, as he had done with the lands of the Appellants. Whatever his plans were, they were set at nought by events in Ireland: by the 27th Mortimer had been dead for six days, killed in a skirmish in County Carlow. Mortimer's death had two important ramifications. It certainly added urgency to Richard's plans for a second expedition to Ireland. But more important was that it considerably lessened any hope that the Mortimer claim to the throne could be substantiated (assuming Richard did not leave a natural successor) in that Edmund, the new Earl of March, was only six years old. By the same token, it boosted the hopes of Gaunt and Bolingbroke.

On 3 February 1399, Lancastrian hopes of the throne devolved upon Bolingbroke with the expected death of Gaunt. In the next few weeks, Richard made three decisions that were to prove fatal to him, although only one can be described as a gratuitous act of folly. This was his reversal on 18 March of his earlier decision on Bolingbroke, whom he now exiled for life and declared his estates forfeit. Almost immediately, he began granting portions of the estate to favoured supporters, although 'only until Bolingbroke or his heir shall sue the same out of the king's hands according to the law of the land'. The implication was that Richard, while determined to crush Bolingbroke, did not wish to convey the impression that it was his intention to visit permanent destruction on his house. His confidence that he could get away with this must have been enhanced by the knowledge that he had Bolingbroke's heir (the future Henry V) in his hands. This act, for which there was no legal ground or other good reason, must have rung the alarm in every aristocratic household.

His second decision was to go ahead with his planned invasion of Ireland. The new Lieutenant, the Duke of Surrey, went ahead and he followed with the main force, transported from a port in South Wales in fifty-six ships, landing at Waterford on 1 June. The admiral of the fleet was Thomas Percy, who successfully organised the conveyance of the king's forces as he had those of Gaunt thirteen years earlier. Richard took with him the bulk of the trained troops loyal to him, including Thomas Percy, whose contingent of thirty-five men at arms and 100 archers was equal to those of the Earls of Salisbury and Gloucester, although much smaller than those of the Dukes of Aumerle and Exeter, each of whom furnished 140 men at arms and respectively 500 and 600 archers.

Richard's third decision, also part of the arrangements for the expedition, was to appoint his uncle, the Duke of York, as Keeper of the Realm. York was, in Chris Given-Wilson's words, 'a political lightweight', but perhaps protocol and precedence required this appointment, and he did have the assistance of four of Richard's most trusted courtiers, the Earl of Wiltshire and the three knights, Bagot, Bussy and Greene. But this only served to underline the fact that the Duke was not a commanding authority or seen as the man for an emergency. At that moment, of course, there was no emergency, although there was enough unrest in the country to merit caution.

The Coup d'État of 1399

Within days of Richard's departure for Ireland with most of his close supporters and reliable troops, Bolingbroke became aware that there was in effect a power vacuum in England. Since his exile, he had been in living in Paris, where the French government, acknowledging the injustice of Richard's treatment of him, received him as an honoured guest. At the same time, they would have recognised his potential as a political pawn. Indeed, behind the courteous façade, Bolingbroke was a prisoner, his ability to return to England entirely dependent upon the goodwill of the French government. And Richard had every reason to believe that the

French government would restrain Bolingbroke: although Anglo-French relations were somewhat tense at this time, Richard's wife was the French king's daughter; and the most powerful man in the government of France was the Duke of Burgundy, who, as Count of Flanders, needed to maintain good commercial relations with England. But at this moment, the Duke of Burgundy was away from Paris. His absence gave freedom of action to his rival, the Duke of Orleans, who for reasons of his own was willing to help Bolingbroke. On 17 June, the two men, for their mutual convenience and advantage, entered into a treaty of friendship and within days Bolingbroke set out for England.

From this point we are dealing with situations and events where the aphorism *quot homines, tot sententiae* (as many opinions as men) applies. Although the various chroniclers who recorded the developing crisis tell broadly the same story, they are at variance in the important details of time, place and motive. Moreover, any attempt to evaluate what they say is bedevilled by the fact that some wrote before the change of regime, some afterwards, while some rewrote what they had written in order to be in harmony with the new political dispensation. In fact, there are no means of judging for certain which of them, if any, is telling the truth. All are suspect on the grounds of bias and/or inaccurate information. Not surprisingly, therefore, historians are far from being in agreement as to precisely what happened and when, and to the motives of the leading participants. Consequently, it becomes necessary to fall back on what is probable and what seems to make most sense, given the circumstances. Ultimately, this lack of a firm foundation of certain evidence is unsatisfactory, but unavoidable. This want of certainty is perhaps one reason why so many historians have been attracted to these events.

When he embarked for England, Bolingbroke had with him a band of supporters who had followed him into exile. It included thirty-seven knights and was sufficiently large to require the use of ten or twelve ships. After sailing from Boulogne, their apparently indecisive movements were either an attempt to keep the opposition guessing, or uncertainty as to the best part of the country in which to make landfall. In the end, they put ashore at Ravenspur (Spurn Head) at the mouth of the River Humber. This may have been their intention all along, since Lancastrian territorial strength lay primarily in Yorkshire, Lancashire and the North Midlands. Nor is the precise date of their landing known. It may have been as early as the last days of June, but certainly no later than 4 July. From the outset, Bolingbroke displayed an ability to make rapid decisions and to act upon them with speed, characteristics that were to be his hallmarks and his salvation during the next few years, ultimately to the detriment of the Percys.

At this point he was playing a very dangerous game: he had come back to England with only a comparatively small band of adherents, uncertain of what support he might receive, but certain that his action would be construed as treason. Yet within thirteen weeks he would have deposed Richard II and become Henry IV. In contrast to those of the recent past, in the events that brought about this conclusion, the Earl and his heir, Hotspur, were to play central and vital roles. As will become apparent, they made the greatest contribution to the military strength, without which nothing would have been possible. But the brains behind so much of what was done, and especially how it was done, were probably less theirs but more those of Thomas Arundel, the deposed but soon to be reinstated Archbishop of Canterbury, who had joined Bolingbroke before his departure from France. This is not to imply a stark contrast, but neither the Earl, who was without doubt well versed in the ways of the political world, nor his son, appear to have had first-rate intellects. This Arundel had by virtue of inborn intelligence, enhanced by legal training and many years of experience in clerical and secular administration. The other mind of quality was undoubtedly that of Bolingbroke himself, who was an intelligent, well-educated man of wide interests.

When Bolingbroke first met the Percys is not certain, but it may have been at Bridlington, within a few days of landing. During the next fortnight, Bolingbroke moved swiftly to secure control of the strategic castles at Pickering, Knaresborough and Pontefract, while at the same time taking the necessary steps to call out the Lancastrian affinity. By 16 July, he was at Doncaster, the gateway to southern England, where the Earl and Hotspur joined him, together with their retinues. If a meeting had taken place at Bridlington, it was probably then that the Percys had indicated a willingness to support Bolingbroke, but it would have taken the intervening days for them to mobilise their retainers. It was also at Doncaster that Bolingbroke's cause was bolstered by the adherence of other powerful northern lords: the Earl of Westmorland; William, Lord Roos; William, Lord Willoughby; and Ralph, Lord Greystock. Assuming the record of payments by Bolingbroke for the wages of troops to be an accurate guide, the military contribution of these men was crucial. Known payments totalled £4,870, of which no less that £1,999, or 41 per cent, went to the two Percys. A further £969, that is, 20 per cent, went to Westmorland, Roos and Willoughby. In all, these five men appear to have furnished Bolingbroke with over 60 per cent of his effective fighting force. The remainder of the money was paid in comparatively small amounts to members of the Lancastrian affinity.

It was at this juncture that the first of the important and tantalising uncertainties occurred. Writing many years later, John Hardyng, at the time a very junior member of Hotspur's household, claimed that at this gathering Bolingbroke swore an oath that his ends were fivefold: to regain his inheritance, that is, his titles and the estates of his father and those he had acquired through his marriage to the heiress, Mary de Bohun (who had died in 1394); to bring Richard under control; to reform the government; to disband the king's hated and feared Cheshire troops; and to ensure that in future taxation was levied only when necessary and with the consent of parliament. By implication, although not overtly stated, he had no designs on the throne. However, the chronicler of Dieulacres Abbey, also writing after Bolingbroke had become Henry IV, explicitly stated that he also swore to the Percys on the holy relics of the Augustinian canonry at Bridlington that he was not aiming for the throne and that he would stand aside if there were any one worthier. The oath was an answer, albeit an ambiguous one, which implicitly defines the question to which it was a response. It is possible, of course, that both statements may be true, but the circumstances different: Bolingbroke may have sworn regarding the Crown privately to the Percys at Bridlington at the outset of his sweep through Yorkshire, while the more innocuous oath was sworn in a wider company at Doncaster.

What are we to make of this? Bolingbroke's five aims present no problem. In effect, they constituted a political reform programme that

111

placed him in line with earlier baronial reform leaders stretching back to the men who forced King John to seal Magna Carta. Any man in such a tight political situation was bound to realise how imperative it was to attract support by issuing a policy manifesto to which few were likely to object. The question of the throne was more problematical, and perhaps went back to 1387, when the Appellants, including Bolingbroke, seriously contemplated deposing Richard. What saved Richard on that occasion was almost certainly the lack of agreement about his replacement. In 1399, the field was less congested. Gloucester was dead, as was Roger Mortimer, leaving an eight-year-old son as his heir. Gaunt had gone from the scene, and York, the last surviving son of Edward III, appears not to have been a man of ambition. For Bolingbroke, the way to the throne would have appeared largely free of obstructions.

And it is hard to believe that, from the outset, he did not have the throne in mind. Given the ruthless way politics had been conducted in the immediate past and the cynical and barefaced duplicity displayed by Richard in his dealings with his political enemies, Bolingbroke could have been in little doubt that it was a case of *aut Caesar, aut nihil.* There was no precedent for an English king being permanently restrained or shackled by a constitutional arrangement devised for that purpose. Once he had regained independence, a man like Richard would sooner or later seek to wreak vengeance on his opponents, as he had done in 1397.

Why did the Percys, father and son, sign up with Bolingbroke? Superficially, the answer is obvious: in their eyes they too had been abused by Richard II in that he had deprived them of that which they so highly prized, the control of the Border zone through the wardenships of the Marches. And it was clear to them that they were incapable of bending him to their will, even with one of their family in such an apparently influential position at court. They must have seen Richard as dangerously untrustworthy and a threat to the interests of everyone outside his coterie. If Bolingbroke, with whose family the Percys had a longstanding association, could with their help restrain the king, then suitable rewards would come their way. Another consideration almost certainly would have been the decision of Ralph Neville, now enhanced in land and in title as Earl of Westmorland, to go with Bolingbroke: for the

Percys to have remained passive would be to risk Neville reaping the rewards they desired.

As regards the question of the Crown, it is less easy to be certain of their attitude. However, if it is true that they put Bolingbroke on the spot in the earliest days of his invasion, it indicates an anxiety that shows the matter was of great concern to them. That it should have been so may well have related to Hotspur's family. Hotspur's wife, Elizabeth, was the eldest daughter of Edmund Mortimer, Third Earl of March and sister of Roger Mortimer, Fourth Earl of March, who was killed in Ireland in the summer of 1398. It was their mother, however, who was the crucial factor, for she was Philippa, the only child of Lionel of Antwerp, Duke of Clarence, the second son of Edward III. If descent via the female was not a bar, then Edmund Mortimer, Fifth Earl of March, Roger Mortimer's son born in 1391, and after him his younger brother, Roger, would have a superior claim to the throne than Bolingbroke, whose father, John of Gaunt, was the third son of Edward III. And should the Fifth Earl of March and his brother die without heirs, arguably their claims would devolve upon Henry Percy, Hotspur's son, born in 1393. Clearly, there are many ifs in this line of argument, but descent via the female was allowed in England, in both law and practice, and, as everyone would have been aware, a century earlier John Balliol's claim to the throne of Scotland was deemed superior to that of Robert Bruce, even though it came through his mother. Bolingbroke would not have been ignorant of any of this, which may explain his shuffling response: who else but Mortimer could he have meant by 'anyone worthier'?

The Earl and his son were in a cleft stick: there were risks if they held back, and serious potential drawbacks if they did not. In their situation, they had no option but to accept Bolingbroke's assurances, whether they believed them or not. Having concluded that action was preferable to inaction, they and their retinues provided the core of Bolingbroke's power as he advanced southwards through the north and west Midlands, frequently through, or close to, the centres of the Lancastrian estate. Meanwhile, the Duke of York did what he could to raise sufficient troops to halt Bolingbroke's progress. Men loyal to Richard were summoned with their retinues and orders were sent to the sheriffs of ten southern counties requiring each to bring out his *posse*. In the end, it is likely that York was able to put together a force of about 3,000 men. His aim seems to have been to move westwards so as to link up with the king, who would be expected to return from Ireland to his port of embarkation in South Wales. Bolingbroke's purpose was therefore to head him off.

The two armies met at Berkeley in Gloucestershire on 27 July, but not to do battle. At a conference held at the church outside Berkeley Castle, York threw in his lot with Bolingbroke. His reasons are not entirely clear. He was not really the fighting sort, and it seems likely that desertions were thinning his hastily assembled force, shire levies especially being unlikely to risk their lives for matters of little direct concern to them. It is also said that York acknowledged the justice of Bolingbroke's claim to have been wrongfully disinherited. This is entirely credible, since, like every other landowner, he too would have recognised the threat Richard posed, even to his own kin. His decision to betray the man who was both his king and his nephew was one of the critical events of the summer. The absence of a royal army would have been a major factor influencing Sir Peter Courtenay's decision two days later to surrender the important castle at Bristol. This delivered three of Richard's most ardent supporters – the Earl of Wiltshire, Sir John Bussy and Sir Henry Green – into Bolingbroke's hands. They were executed after a 'trial' before what was scarcely more than a 'kangaroo court' presided over by the Earl, who Bolingbroke had appointed constable of his army.

By now Richard's cause was close to being lost, yet it was only around this time that he arrived back in South Wales, despite having learned of Bolingbroke's arrival in England about two weeks earlier. There is, and probably always will be, uncertainty about his actions during these days, although Dorothy Johnston's research has gone a long way to clarify the picture. It is clear that in one respect he reacted promptly by despatching the Earl of Salisbury to raise forces in North Wales and the Palatine of Chester: Salisbury is known to have arrived and taken command at Chester by 19 July. On the other hand, he delayed his own return from Ireland to South Wales and this has long defied satisfactory explanation. Johnston's use of administrative records led her to the conclusion that the king and his magnates each made his own arrangements, which had to be *ad hoc*, since the ships that had brought them had been paid off. Consequently, Richard's army embarked in fragmented groups from several Irish ports and landed in many places in South Wales and south-west England. The best estimate for Richard's own landing is at either Milford or Haverfordwest on 24 July. He then set up camp at Pembroke, but it was not feasible for him to attempt to move until he had managed to reassemble his dispersed forces. This necessary delay, together with news or rumours of Bolingbroke's progess and the Duke of York's defection, appears to have led to desertions.

It was this crumbling situation that almost certainly explains Richard's decision to flee Pembroke on 1 August, accompanied by his closest companions, the Dukes of Exeter and Surrey, the Earl of Gloucester, three bishops and what remained of his bodyguard. His destination was North Wales, where he had every reason to expect to find a large army under Salisbury's command. With the king gone, Thomas Percy ordered the other officers of the royal household to deposit what they had in their keeping in Carmarthen Castle. He then publicly broke his staff of office, thus formally and publicly signalling that the household was disbanded. Immediately after this act, he went to join Bolingbroke at Bristol, where by 6 August he was acting as Admiral of England.

It is impossible to know whether Thomas Percy was privy to Richard's decision or surprised by it. Strictly speaking, unless he had been formally released from office, his was an act of treachery. On the other hand, if Richard had kept Percy in ignorance of his intention, it could be argued that the king had deserted his Steward, not *vice versa*. But these were points of legal and chivalric nicety that were too delicate for such a dangerous situation. It would have been clear to Percy, the experienced politician, that Richard was in deep trouble and that it was now *sauve qui peut*. The most sensible thing for him to do was to join the winning side while there was still time.

While Richard and his small party were struggling to cover the 150 miles of difficult terrain between Carmarthen and Conwy, Bolingbroke was making a triumphal progress northwards from Bristol, via Berkeley, Ross, Hereford, Leominster, Ludlow, Shrewsbury and Holt. He reached Chester, which like Bristol did not put up any resistance, on 9 August. His strategy was entirely sensible, to prevent Richard creating a redoubt in his favourite Principality of Chester, which was now his only hope of salvation. As he set out on this march, he conferred the Wardenship of the West March on the Earl, using the Duchy of Lancaster seal to authenticate the appointment. This was on 2 August and it is likely that it was on the same occasion that he made Thomas Percy Admiral of England. Clearly, both parties now felt confident enough to start showing their hands: Bolingbroke was beginning to act as though he were king; and the Earl was willing enough to go along with this in order to start reaping the reward for which he had joined up.

Richard arrived in North Wales about the same time as Bolingbroke reached Chester. There he came across another calamity. Although Salisbury had managed to raise an army, and it may have been a large one, without the presence of the king, and with rumours that he was dead beginning to circulate, the troops rapidly melted away. Salisbury, with a minute remainder, retreated to Conwy. Bereft of any military power, Richard had no option but to retreat. He sent the Dukes of Surrey and Exeter to discover Bolingbroke's intentions: ominously, they did not return.

It was now that another unsolvable mystery surrounding the Earl developed. On 10 August, he was commissioned by Bolingbroke to go to Richard at Conwy to persuade him to surrender. Some accounts claim that Archbishop Arundel accompanied him, but this is almost certainly not true. What he did take with him was a sizeable number of his retainers, the majority of whom, however, he left on the east side of the Conwy estuary, well out of sight of the castle. Since his interview with Richard was private, it is not possible to be fully confident about its course. However, it seems probable that the Earl insisted to Richard that Bolingbroke had only three demands: the restoration of his inheritance; a Parliament for the reformation of the government, presided over by himself in his capacity as hereditary Steward of England; and the trial for treason of seven men, including the Dukes of Surrey and Exeter and the Earl of Salisbury. The Earl, it was said, swore on the consecrated Host that this was the sum of Bolingbroke's demands and that he had no designs on the throne. The alternative versions, which have Richard agreeing to relinquish his crown, are wholly implausible.

It took Richard three days to decide that he had no option but to leave the shelter of Conwy and to accompany the Earl to meet Bolingbroke. He must have been uncertain and fearful about the worth of the Earl's guarantee. For us, the uncertainty is whether the Earl was deliberately lying. Had he simply retailed to Richard what Bolingbroke had insisted to him, or had he been left to use whatever means he thought fit to get Richard out of Conwy Castle and into Bolingbroke's hands? Given that Richard's capacity for deceit and duplicity was known to all involved, it is hard to believe that Bolingbroke and the Earl were not being cynically deceptive in their approach. Both men knew that the stakes were of the highest and that possession of the king's person was vital: dirty tricks were in order.

Richard capitulated on 15 August, and the small party set out across the Conwy Estuary. Shortly beyond its eastern bank, they came across the main body of the Earl's armed retinue, the sight of which, not surprisingly, filled Richard with alarm. To reassure him, the Earl again swore on a consecrated Host that neither he nor Bolingbroke had deceived him. That evening the party reached the castle at Flint. Early the following morning, Bolingbroke arrived from Chester with his army and surrounded the castle. With Bolingbroke were Thomas Percy and his nephew, Hotspur, who was described by Jean Creton (a young Frenchman travelling with Richard's court) as one of Bolingbroke's main captains and the best knight in England, a testimony to the younger Percy's reputation. As he stood on the battlements of the castle, Richard could no longer be in doubt that his freedom was at an end.

Nevertheless, the courtesies were observed. The Earl persuaded Bolingbroke not to enter the castle until Richard had eaten, and then to come in with only a small number of his people. When they met, Bolingbroke assured Richard that he intended him no harm and that his wish was to assist him to be a better ruler. However, the true nature of Richard's situation was made clear to him by the simple fact of his being provided with a nag for his ride to Chester. From there Bolingbroke, his captive and the three Percys set out for London on 20 August. With the king in his hands, Bolingbroke was sufficiently confident to dismiss the bulk of his army, despite an attempt by Cheshire men to free Richard near Nantwich.

Their progress was through Stafford, Lichfield, Coventry, Northampton, Dunstable and St Albans, finally reaching London by 1 September, when Richard was committed to the Tower. Bolingbroke now exposed his intention to depose Richard by setting up a commission to see how this could best be done. In addition, from 10 September he ceased dating the documents he uttered by Richard's regal year, using *anno domini* dates instead.

It took until the end of the month for arguments to be settled and tactics agreed. How much the Percys contributed to this is uncertain, but because of the legal subtleties that had to be considered and the intellectual arguments that had to be contrived, it is more likely that men such as Archbishop Arundel and the Chief Justice, Sir William Thirning, had a much larger input. Both the agreement and the forensic skills of the latter were particularly needed. Nevertheless, when it came to treating with the king, the Earl as the most senior lay nobleman in Bolingbroke's entourage and the holder of the office of Constable had a leading role.

The problem to be solved had two inextricably linked parts: how legitimately to remove Richard from the throne; and who to put in his place. As regards the first, the solution ultimately adopted was to cajole Richard into abdicating, but also to depose him for bad government. Evidence of the latter required the mental efforts of a commission, which in the end produced a list of thirty-three charges. The remarkable thing about these is that they did not contain the wildly improbable allegations of gross immorality usually found in most similar medieval lists. All related closely to Richard's actions, so that, although biased, they had a basic truth. They are a testimony to the range of criticism to which Richard's style of government had exposed him.

The last act was played out in the Tower and then in Parliament, which had been summoned in Richard's name at the beginning of the month. On Sunday, 28 September, a deputation led by the Earl went to the Tower with the aim of securing Richard's agreement to abdicate. The various accounts of what happened conflict, some even suggesting that he resigned cheerfully and willingly. This is scarcely credible: Richard placed such a high value on his status as an anointed monarch that it is unlikely that he would relinquish it, except under duress. In the end, he agreed, but on condition that Bolingbroke came to see him before he did so. The meeting took place the following day. It is possible that Richard hoped that this would result in an arrangement that would leave him as titular king while giving the rule of the country and the guarantee of the succession to Bolingbroke. There was a very recent precedent for this in Scotland, where Robert III, having admitted to misgovernment, agreed to continue as the wearer of the crown, leaving the exercise of royal authority to his eldest son, David, Duke of Rothesay. If Richard had hoped for a similar arrangement, he was disappointed. All he was granted was his life.

The final scene took place at a meeting of Parliament in Westminster Hall, where the throne stood empty, covered with cloth of gold. Richard's resignation was announced, followed by his deposition on the basis of the thirty-three articles. Then Bolingbroke stepped forward and claimed the throne in a short but ambiguous speech, delivered in English. In it, he stressed his descent from Henry III, emphasised Richard's failures as a ruler and mentioned the speed with which the country had welcomed him. The first part hinted at a claim to the throne based upon hereditary right, while in the last part he seemed to suggest 'right of conquest', an argument that the Chief Justice had earlier advised against, as setting too obvious a precedent. The Earl and John Norbury, an esquire but one of the most trusted members of Bolingbroke's retinue, then formally asked the lords individually whether they agreed that Bolingbroke should be king. There were no objections or abstentions. It was Thomas Percy, no doubt wishing to emphasise his transfer of loyalty, who then stepped forward and shouted 'Long live Henry of Lancaster, King of England'.

In the early days of October, the Earl was again in action, when, with another stalwart Lancastrian, Sir Thomas Erpingham, he went to meet the Convocation of the Province of Canterbury to assure them that, as king, Bolingbroke would respect the liberties of the church, not tax the clergy, except in dire necessity in wartime, and would take a strong line against heresy, an assurance they needed in the light of Bolingbroke's father's espousal of John Wycliffe. It is significant that on both occasions the Earl was accompanied by a long-serving and totally trusted member of Bolingbroke's retinue, each man, it would seem, representing one of the two halves of Bolingbroke's support.

Henry IV's coronation took place on 13 October, the feast of Edward the Confessor, a bitter and presumably intentional irony in that the penultimate Old English king was Richard II's favourite saint. Four swords were carried before Henry in procession to Westminster Abbey, the Earl bearing that worn by Bolingbroke when he landed at Ravenspur. This was clearly an honour, but it may also have been a move on Henry's part to ensure that the Earl publicly and formally acknowledged the legitimacy of the deposition and usurpation. If it is true that Hotspur did not attend the coronation feast (an unsubstantiated allegation), Henry's caution was justified. But there is no other trustworthy evidence that at this stage the Percys were opposed to Bolingbroke becoming Henry IV; nor is there any evidence that they raised the issue of the rights of the young Edmund Mortimer. The only hint of his potential presence as a spectre at the feast was in the wording of Henry's claim to the throne before Parliament, when notably he failed to present himself as Richard's undisputed heir. In fact, the only source to claim that the Percys attempted to prevent Boling-broke's taking the throne is John Hardyng, the long-time Percy adherent, writing many years later. It was in the second version of his account, penned for Edward IV, whose right to the throne stemmed from the Mortimer line, that Hardyng claimed that all three Percys tried to persuade Bolingbroke to keep his oath, but were unable to coerce him into doing so, because at his request they had sent the bulk of their troops home. It is safe to dismiss this account as, in modern parlance, 'spin'.

What appears to be beyond resolution is the question of their real attitude to the turn of events. It may be that they were perfectly willing to see Bolingbroke on the throne, knowing that his debt to them would require massive reward, and that the claims of Edmund Mortimer were of little moment in comparison. However, given Hotspur's close connection with the house of Mortimer, it seems hard to believe that he at least would have been totally indifferent to those claims. It may be that the tide of events had run so swiftly in Bolingbroke's favour that they were simply unable to do anything but be swept along by it. It is also possible that Bolingbroke deceived them until it was too late for them to deflect him from his chosen course. But this is improbable: they were too well versed in the ways of their world not to know or suspect what was afoot.

What the new king's long-term intentions were as regards his pre-decessor is uncertain. Initially, he seems to have planned to keep him alive, but in close confinement. That this was an unrealistic policy was almost immediately revealed by the plot by a group of Richard's supporters, headed by the Earls of Huntingdon, Kent, Rutland (who had been deprived of their recently acquired dukedoms) and Salisbury to murder Henry and his family at Windsor during the Christmas festivities and then to release and restore Richard. Their scheme was betrayed by the Earl of Rutland and quickly dealt with. Richard was promptly moved to Ponte-fract Castle in Yorkshire, where he is known to have died by mid-February 1400. Whether he was murdered, a course of action urged by the Earl, or starved himself to death in a state of depression, is probably an unsolvable mystery.

In the days and months following the start of the new reign, the Percys collected their rewards. Thomas Percy retained his title as Earl of Worcester and was confirmed as Admiral of England, a post to which he was well fitted by his previous experiences in the role and of war at sea. Although he was required to relinquish the land he had been granted by Richard II from the estates of the Duke of Gloucester and the Earl of Arundel, whose heirs were rightfully allowed to regain them, he was compensated by having all other Crown grants confirmed and a generous annuity of 700 marks (£466.67) a year. He had made his switch of allegiance at the right moment and his wide-ranging abilities and political skills were too valuable to be discarded. And in the years immediately following, he was an active member of the Council and was used in diplomatic negotiations with France over several matters, notably the return of Richard II's child queen, Isabelle, and in the arrangements for Henry's marriage to Joan, the widow of the Duke of Brittany. He was also engaged militarily in his capacity as Admiral, leading a naval force to Bordeaux to inhibit French threats to Aquitaine.

The Earl fared equally well. Before the reign had begun, he had secured the prized Wardenship of the West March, which carried an annual fee of £1,600 in peacetime and £6,000 in time of war. To this was added the Lordship of Man and the office of Constable of England. But it was his heir, Hotspur, who made the greatest gains. He regained the Wardenship of the East March, the annual fees being set at £3,000 in time of peace and £12,000 in the event of war. In addition, he was granted the largest Crown property in Northumberland, the lordship and castle of Bamburgh. All this meant that between them, the Earl and his son controlled the crucial offices on the English side of the Border. But Hotspur also acquired similar power on the Scottish side: as Warden of the East March he was also Captain of Berwick, to which was added the post of Captain of Roxburgh. Together with the family's interests in and around Jedburgh, these placed the major offices in the Scottish Border country in Hotspur's hands. Although not so styled, Hotspur was in effect viceroy in respect of the land between the Tyne and the Lammermuir Hills. His father did not enjoy quite the same degree of success in the West March, in that Ralph Neville, Earl of Westmorland's brother, Thomas, Lord Furnival, was granted Lochmaben and Annandale for life.

Nor were Hotspur's gains solely in the Border zones. He was appointed Justice of North Wales and also Justice of Chester, which included the county of Flint. In these roles he was head of the administration of both jurisdictions, although the latter was not so extensive as Richard's Principality of Chester, which was abolished and the Arundel lands restored to the young earl, the son of Richard Fitzalan executed in 1398. He also was given the constableships of the important castles of Chester, Flint, Conwy and Caernafon and the lordship of Anglesey, with its castle at Beaumaris. In very large measure, he was given control of Richard II's heartland. Moreover, the Earl was granted custody during his minority of the lands of young Edmund Mortimer, Fifth Earl of March, which included the county of Denbigh separating the palatinates of Chester and North Wales, as well several large blocks of territory in central Wales. Together, these grants complemented those to Thomas Percy in South Wales, thereby making the Percy family virtual viceroys in Wales. Arguably, Hotspur's links with the Mortimer family, and the claims of that family to the throne, made the extension of Percy power into Wales a risky move. It may be, of course, that Henry recognised that the Percys, with their proven ability to succeed in the turbulent situation in the Border zone, were the right people to cope with a difficult part of his realm. But it did mean that the Percys had come close to being all-powerful in the two regions that were only semi-attached to the main body of the kingdom.

For the Percys, the consequences of the revolution of 1399 were that the Earl of Northumberland and his son, Hotspur, were the dominant men in the Anglo-Scottish Border zone, in terms of both office and estate, and that Hotspur and his uncle, Thomas Percy, Earl of Worcester, controlled the administration of Wales, while the Earl had the custody of the Welsh estate of Hotspur's nephew. They had made no gains in the heartlands of the English realm, south of the Trent and east of the Severn, but it is doubtful whether they had looked to do so. The Earl and his heir were men of the periphery. One further point is worth making: when the rewards to the Percys are viewed in perspective, Hotspur appears as the chief beneficiary, an indication, perhaps, that the younger generation was taking over the leadership role, a notion reinforced by what followed.

FIVE

Hubris: Three Rebellions, 1399–1408

It is hard to conceive what else the Percys realistically could have expected to gain from their help, crucial though it was, in turning Henry of Bolingbroke, Duke of Lancaster into King Henry IV. Yet, less than four years later, they launched (for them) the first of three disastrous rebellions against him, which in a five-year period brought utter, albeit temporary, ruin to the family. Although the course of events is clear enough on all three occasions, the reasons why the Percys became so bitter or frustrated or disillusioned with the king they had helped to make cannot be perceived with complete confidence. Consequently, what follows is more certain in description than in explanation. This said, a number of events and developments may be identified as the causes of the rising hostility of the Percys to Henry IV, although none in itself appears to have been so serious as to have warranted armed rebellion. It is to their cumulative effect, therefore, combined with the characters and personalities of the three Percys, that we should look for understanding. The influential events took place not only in England, but also in Scotland, where disturbed political conditions led to renewed military aggression, and more particularly in Wales, which had been peaceful since the Edwardian conquest of the late thirteenth century.

Discontent

In England, it was changes in government that induced Percy disquiet and discontent. Alan Rogers has argued that at the outset of his reign, Henry IV filled most of the important state offices with men with no national standing, whose appeal was that they were well known to him and trusted by him as a result of their work for himself or his father. This attempt at very personal and exclusive government produced an adverse reaction in the Parliament of 1401, resulting in their removal and replacement by men of higher social status and greater experience of government, many of whom had served Richard II in the 1390s. The main driving force behind these changes appears to have been the Percys, so that when the Parliament was dissolved at the end of March they were dominant in the administration and also the royal household, where Thomas Percy was reappointed as Steward of the Household. Clearly, they were prepared to resist any attempt on Henry's part to have an exclusively personal administration.

But Henry, like previous kings, was not prepared to accept this constraint, and over the next two years, he gradually changed the personnel of his administration by bringing in men of his own preference, notably Henry Beaufort, Bishop of Lincoln, and Henry Bowet, Bishop of Bath and Wells as, respectively, Chancellor and Treasurer. More significantly, Thomas Percy was replaced as Steward of the Household, a change that sharply reduced the Percy potential for influencing royal decisions. Beaufort was one of the king's half-brothers, being a son of John of Gaunt by his third wife, Katherine Swynford. Another Beaufort also became a member of the king's inner circle: John Beaufort, Earl of Somerset, Henry Beaufort's elder brother. In 1399, he had been very close to Richard, so much so that his was the largest contingent in the force raised by the Duke of York to oppose Henry's invasion. He was so identified with Richard's cause that the Percys pressed for his execution. Henry, however, rejected their urgings, although he did strip him of the title of Marquis (of Dorset) on the grounds that it was a foreign novelty associated with the previous regime. As early as February 1400, he appointed him to the post of Great Chamberlain and thereafter he became one of Henry's closest collaborators: Alastair Dunn claims that he was Henry's 'chief of staff' until his death in 1410.

But probably a more threatening aspect to Percy interests, certainly in the north, was Henry's promotion of Ralph Neville, who, like Thomas Percy, was allowed to retain his Ricardian title, Earl of Westmorland. Neville's first wife, Margaret, daughter of the Earl of Stafford, died on 9 June 1396, and within weeks he married Joan Beaufort, the the widow of Sir Robert Ferrers. The true significance of his marriage was that his new wife was the half-sister of the king and the full sister of the Earl of Somerset and the Bishop of Lincoln. This astute move firmly aligned him with the Lancastrian cause.

In return for Neville's active support during the summer of 1399, Henry rewarded him with the office of Marshal, the grant of the Honour of Richmond for life and the wardship of the Dacre estate in Cumberland. His brother, Thomas, Lord Furnival, was also rewarded with the grant of Lochmaben and Annandale. Douglas Biggs has underlined how important the Richmond grant was. Not only did this increase his annual income by a massive £1,500; when added to the property he already had there it made him a major power in the North Riding of Yorkshire. His territorial and income enhancement, together with his appointment as Marshal, put him on a par with the Earl, nationally and regionally. Superficially, these favours were rewards for services rendered, but they also marked a return to Richard II's policy of promoting Ralph Neville as a counterweight to the Percys in the Border zone. The Percys could hardly have regarded them otherwise, and their concern would have been heightened by two further changes in 1402: the Keepership of Roxburgh, which had been granted to Hotspur for life, was taken from him and handed over to the Earl of Westmorland; and Thomas Percy was replaced as Steward of the Royal Household by one of Westmorland's retainers, William Heron, Lord Say.

The third aspect of Henry's government, which undoubtedly caused tension between him and the Earl and Hotspur, was financial. Both men were increasingly frustrated by the king's refusal to pay in full the fees due to them. The extent to which these complaints were justified is not easy to perceive, since it is not possible to be certain exactly how much was owed to the Percys. J.M.W. Bean believes that it was much less than the £20,000 they claimed, but recently Cynthia Neville has argued that Henry deliberately withheld payment to the Percys while settling promptly with Ralph Neville, so adding insult to injury. Whatever the truth, there is no doubt that the Percys felt strongly that they were being short-changed and that in consequence they were being forced to finance their duties out of their own pockets.

On the other hand, there is equally no doubt that Henry's financial problems were real and pressing. These were due in part to the extraordinary expense (amounting to £18,000 in 1402) of trying to suppress the revolt in Wales (see below), repulsing Scottish incursions and maintaining control of the Channel. This was on top of the normal peacetime costs of garrisons in Calais, Bordeaux and Ireland, which consumed nearly £30,000. But what really ate into Henry's income, which amounted to about £130,000, was the annual disbursement of £24,000 in the form of the annuities he granted with the aim of enlarging his retinue, thereby widening the base of his support. This is understandable, given his dubious constitutional position and the continuing rumours of Richard's existence, but it was widely seen as an unnecessary extravagance in a man who had trumpeted his intention to live within his income. The Percys may have resented this prodigal outlay aimed at securing support that would be passive for the most part, while they, who were actively defending the kingdom, were being denied their dues.

Henry's problem with Scotland was partly of his own making, but in part it stemmed from political conflicts north of the Border arising from the weak kingship of Robert III. The most disruptive of these was the quarrel between the Earls of March and Douglas that came to a head in 1400. Its cause went back to 1395, when Robert III's heir, David, Earl of Carrick (who became Duke of Rothesay in 1398), married Elizabeth, the daughter of George Dunbar, Earl of March. The union was irregular in that the couple were within the forbidden degrees of consanguinity and the necessary papal dispensation had not been secured. Moreover, it seems that the match was not to Robert III's liking and was arranged without proper consultation with either him or the Scottish Parliament. The upshot was an annulment, but with the understanding that there would be a remarriage after a suitable interval. But in 1400, the Third Earl of Douglas (known as Archibald the Grim) secured the marriage of Rothesay to his daughter, Mary. Dunbar was unable to obtain any redress, not even the return of the money he had paid for his daughter's dowry. His response was extreme but understandable: he renounced his allegiance to Robert III and crossed the Border with his family and some of his affinity to take service with the King of England.

This, together with the successful Scottish raid on Wark on Tweed in October 1399, may have helped to persuade Henry to undertake what proved to be an expensive and apparently fruitless expedition into Scotland in August 1400. His army was very large by the standards of the time, totalling 13,000 fighting troops. Here it is worth noting that the Earl's contingent was modest: seven men at arms and 160 archers, less that the average contribution of the earls involved and in marked contrast to the 200 men at arms and 1,000 archers furnished by Neville. What should be read into this is not certain, but it does look like a snub that served to underline the status of the Earl of Westmorland as a major factor in Border affairs. Thomas Percy was not involved militarily, having been detailed to remain in London to attend Council meetings.

The expedition achieved nothing substantial: as usual, the Scots had more sense than to offer battle, and Henry had neither the time nor the resources to stay long enough in Edinburgh to force Rothesay to make the gesture he sought. The whole affair lasted less than a month. The reasons behind it remain a matter of speculation. Henry's avowed aim was to wring out of the Scottish government an acknowledgement of the age-old English claim to feudal overlordship of Scotland, which he may have felt would help to bolster his dubious title. But he may also have seen it as an opportunity of underlining to the Percys that the ultimate authority in the Border zone was his.

For the Percys, the crucial events took place in 1402, and in them the exiled Scottish Earl of March played an influential part. March and the Percys began raiding north of the Tweed in 1400, with Douglas adherents and those of March's affinity who had failed to join him in England as their main targets. A raid led by March and Hotspur was defeated in the late winter of 1401. But on 22 June 1402, March had his revenge. With the Berwick garrison, he inflicted a severe defeat at Nisbet Muir, near Duns in Berwickshire, on one of his erstwhile adherents, Patrick Hepburn of Hailes (near East Linton), who was returning from a raid into Northumberland. No fewer than 240 of the 400 men of the Scottish force, including Hepburn, were killed or captured, significantly weakening the fighting strength of Lothian.

By this date the political situation in Scotland had become less stable. At the end of 1400, Archibald, Third Earl of Douglas died and was succeeded as Fourth Earl by his son, Archibald, who came to be known as the

Tyneman (Loser). Then between October 1401 and March 1402 Robert, Duke of Albany, the king's brother, arrested, imprisoned and finally starved to death his nephew, the king's elder son and heir-apparent, David, Duke of Rothesay. In January 1399, Rothesay had been appointed king's lieutenant for three years, but had exercised his role so aggressively that Albany's political power was seriously undermined. The murder of Rothesay gave Albany control of the Scottish government, but at the expense of reliance upon the support of the new Earl of Douglas. Douglas's ambition was to gain possession of the estates of the exiled Earl of March and thereby establish his domination of the Scottish East March. In return for Douglas's acceptance of his *coup d'état*, Albany agreed to support Douglas's plan to avenge Nisbet Muir and destroy March by commiting his military resources to a major raid into Northumberland. When assembled, the army may have numbered, initially at least, 10,000 men. It was nominally under the command of Albany's eldest son, Murdoch Stewart, Earl of Fife and included contingents raised by the Earls of Douglas, Angus and Moray, and also a group of French knights who had come to Scotland following an agreement negotiated a few months earlier.

It was therefore a major *chevauchée* that in late August swept through Northumberland as far as the Tyne, and may have crossed into Durham, although this seems unlikely. While the English government was aware of the Scottish preparations in early August, no attempt was made to impede the southward progress of the invasion. This may have been a tactical decision, but more likely it was the result of the time needed to assemble a force of equivalent size. In command, *ex officio* as Warden of the East March, was Hotspur. With him were his father, the Earl, George Dunbar, Earl of March, who had entered into a military contract with Henry IV, Ralph, Lord Greystoke, Sir Ralph Eure and Sir Henry Fitzhugh, three of the most active men in Border defence. The town of Newcastle also furnished a contingent.

Hotspur's force intercepted the returning Scots, by this time encumbered with booty and perhaps reduced in number by death and desertion, at Humbleton, a few hundred yards north of the small town of Wooler, in Glendale. It was 14 September. The Scottish army took up position on the

130

lower slopes of Humbleton Hill, on a field known today as Red Riggs. As this faces north east, the English army may have mustered at Berwick with the express intention of effecting an interception. Although the Scots had the benefit of the upper ground, their lack of archers was a distinct disadvantage. Although the long spears with which their common soldiers were equipped could be used to form an impenetrable hedgehog or schiltron, this was a defensive formation vulnerable to well-directed archery.

The outcome of the battle was largely decided by two decisions, both taken by Scotsmen. The first was by George Dunbar, Earl of March, who is said to have dissuaded Hotspur from launching an uphill charge with his men at arms against the Scottish schiltron, but, at least initially, to use his archers to disrupt, demoralise and thin the Scottish ranks. The success of this tactic prompted the second decision, by the Lothian knight, Sir John Swinton, one of Douglas's leading Border adherents. Frustrated by the hail of arrows, he gathered a group of around 100 knights and esquires for a downhill charge, in the hope of smashing the English formation. Whether this was a unilateral action or was sanctioned by the Scottish commanders is not clear.

There followed a classic, confused hand-to-hand melée, in which the Scots were defeated. As always, by far the greater number of deaths occurred during the pursuit of the defeated force as it fled the battle, many of them by drowning in the Rivers Till and Tweed. Only seven members of the Scottish armigerous class lost their lives, and none was above the rank of knight. Of much greater long-term importance were the captives. These included the five earls who had led the invasion and at least thirty Scottish knights, most of them from the Border and Lothian regions, as well as a number of the visiting French knights.

It was the fate of these men that shortly became the occasion of a bitter quarrel between the king and Hotspur. A week after the battle, on receipt of the news of the victory (delivered by one of the Earl's esquires, Nicholas Merbury, for which he was granted a generous annual pension of £40), which was in sharp contrast to his own failure to win anything in Wales (see below), Henry wrote to the Earl as Warden of the West March, strictly ordering that none of the Scottish prisoners should be ransomed or released, except on his authority. The stated reason for this prohibition was the 'urgent causes now moving the king', but without indicating what they were. Similar letters were sent to Hotspur as Warden of the East March, George Dunbar, Earl of March, Lord Greystock, Sir Henry Fitzhugh as King's Lieutenant in Roxburgh and Sir Ralph Eure, as Constable of Dunstanburgh Castle. The Earl complied with this order, and on 20 October in the White Hall at Westminster, in a theatrical ceremony, he presented the Earl of Fife, three of the leading Scots and three French knights to the king. Hotspur, however, refused to hand over the Earl of Douglas. In doing so, he flouted the rules of war, which accorded the king the right, for obvious political reasons, to captured commanders and prisoners of royal blood, on the understanding (which Henry explicitly gave in his letters) that he would suitably compensate the captor.

Why Hotspur acted as he did and broke the rule, of which he would have been well aware, is understandable only if it is seen as a direct riposte to the king's refusal to allow him to ransom his brother-in-law, Sir Edmund Mortimer (see below). Otherwise, we are thrust back on the almost private nature of the long-running conflict between the Douglas and Percy families, which had its roots in the early fourteenth century, or an urgent need for the ransom money to solve his own financial problems. He may also have resented Henry's intrusion, which he may have seen as clouding his moment of triumph in avenging his defeat at Otterburn at the hands of the Second Earl of Douglas fourteen years earlier. Whatever the reason, the matter ended in stalemate, Hotspur continuing to hold on to his prisoner, while obeying the king's injunction not to ransom him. The story that Henry and Hotspur quarrelled in public about the issue and that Henry drew his dagger, leading Hotspur to storm out crying 'not here, but in the field' seems too nicely and suitably dramatic to be true.

But Henry's Scottish problem was relatively slight compared with that posed by Wales, which was to remain serious for almost ten years. At its core was Owain Glyn Dŵr, lord of Glyndyfrdwy and Cynllaith in North Wales, whose rebellion has been the subject of detailed analysis by Rees Davies. Although only a landowner on a modest scale, Glyn Dŵr, could claim descent from two ancient Welsh royal families. On 16 September 1400, he raised the standard of revolt, a move apparently triggered by a quarrel with a neighbouring English landowner, Reginald, Lord Grey of Ruthin. The issue between them probably involved disputed land, but

Grey was also alleged to have delayed the delivery of the summons to Glyn Dŵr to join the Scottish expedition, so that his failure to appear would seem treasonous. Beneath and behind these immediate matters, however, were long-festering discontents about the situation in Wales, which were the real reasons for Glyn Dŵr's revolt. It was no sudden whim. The revolt began with an attack on Ruthin on 18 September, when Glyn Dŵr was proclaimed Prince of Wales. Further attacks were then made on other English towns in North Wales, but on 24 September, his forces suffered a defeat at the hands of a locally raised army commanded by Hugh Burnell.

Although a setback, this defeat did not end the revolt; and neither did Henry IV's first expedition into Wales, which, like that into Scotland, cost a great deal of money but produced no result. Like the Scots, the Welsh declined to engage in pitched battles, where the English forces would enjoy marked superiority, but relied on the hostile terrain, the inclement weather and guerrilla attacks. In 1401, Glyn Dŵr had further successes. On 1 April

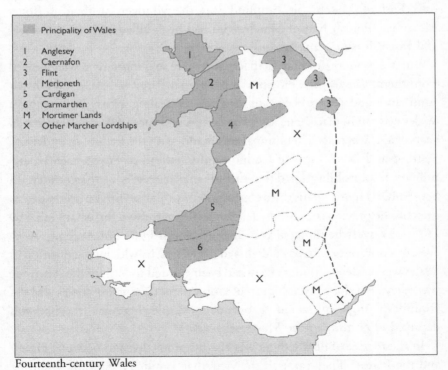

Fourteenth-century Wales

1401, he captured Conwy Castle in a surprise attack, much to Hotspur's embarrassment. It was recovered towards the end of May, but Glyn Dŵr underlined the intractability of the problem he posed by frustrating Henry's second expedition into Wales later in that summer.

As in the case of Scotland, the events of 1402 proved to be critical for the relationship of the king and the Percys. In March, Henry responded to the growing seriousness of the situation by appointing Hotspur as King's Lieutenant in North Wales and Thomas Percy as King's Lieutenant in South Wales. At that moment the Percys seemed to be more firmly in control. But these promotions turned out to be the prelude to disaster. In April, Glyn Dŵr captured his personal enemy, Lord Grey of Ruthin. Then on 22 June, the day the George Dunbar, the Scottish Earl of March, won the engagement at Nisbet Muir, Glyn Dŵr's forces won a bloody battle at Bryn Glas, south of Knighton in Radnorshire, in which they captured Sir Edmund Mortimer, the uncle of young Edmund Mortimer, Fifth (English) Earl of March. Sir Edmund was the younger brother of Roger Mortimer, Fourth Earl of March, who had been killed in Ireland in 1398, and thus Hotspur's brother-in-law.

But it was not the military setbacks that were so important as what flowed from them. On 26 July, Hotspur and Thomas Percy were relieved of their commands and a more elaborate structure for dealing with the problems in Wales was put in place. The king's son, Henry, Prince of Wales, now fifteen years of age, was placed in nominal command, with the Earls of Arundel and Stafford and Lords Grey of Codnor and Charlton of Powys each having military responsibility for different but smaller sectors of the country. In September, Henry led his third expedition into Wales, with no more success than on the previous occasions, a failure that was thrown into sharp relief by Hotspur's overwhelming success at Humbleton Hill. This sacking, however, was only one of the royal slights to the Percys, by which their position in Wales was eroded. Although they had been granted to him for life, Hotspur was relieved of the constableships of Conwy and Caernafon castles and the County of Anglesey, including Beaumaris Castle. Likewise, the Earl was deprived of custody of the Mortimer lands.

In the matter of policy there was also a serious division between Henry and the Percys. They came to the view that a military solution would be difficult if not impossible to achieve. Instead, they favoured trying to achieve a negotiated settlement that would allow Glyn Dŵr to save face. To Henry, however, Glyn Dŵr was a traitor who must be pursued to destruction. Between 1401 and 1403, first Thomas and then the Earl acted as intermediaries in an attempt to achieve a peaceful settlement. This search culminated in Hotspur's agreement with Glyn Dŵr to suspend military activity for three months to see if negotiations could succeed. When Hotspur presented this at court, it was summarily rejected and he was condemned for not using the meeting to seize Glyn Dŵr as a convicted traitor.

There was, of course, more to this than unbiased differences over the best solution to a problem. Behind it was Henry's refusal to allow Hotspur to ransom his brother-in-law, the more galling since Henry had been quick to arrange the ransom of Lord Grey of Ruthin. The royal motive was patently political. It suited Henry well that the acting head of the one family with arguably a better claim to the throne than his should remain a prisoner in enemy hands, while he held the person of the young head of that family, who would not come of age until 1412. Dynastically, Henry now held most of the cards. But not all: even as a prisoner, Sir Edmund Mortimer still had some freedom of action, which he used to some effect. In November 1402, he married Catrin, one of Glyn Dŵr's daughters, it must be assumed to cement a political alliance. By failing to allow Mortimer to be ransomed, Henry had pushed Edmund Mortimer into an alliance with his enemy and thereby had linked the Percys, and Hotspur in particular, to Owain Glyn Dŵr and the nationalist cause in Wales.

Rebellion, 1403

This, then, was the situation in the early months of 1403: in various ways Henry IV had managed to offend, to anger and to thwart all three Percys. But there was nothing to indicate that relations were so far deteriorated that individually or collectively they were close to rebellion. Indeed, in the late winter of 1403 the king made what appears to have been a conciliatory move: on 2 March, he granted the bulk of the Douglas estate, comprising Eskdale, Liddesdale, Lauderdale, Teviotdale, Selkirk and Ettrick Forest, to the Earl and his heirs. This, combined with the fact that he did not press Hotspur for possession of the Earl of Douglas, suggests that he was prepared to conciliate the Percys for the sake of harmony as well as allowing them to attempt to turn southern Scotland into an English-dominated buffer zone. In real terms, of course, what he gave was not his to give. As he saw it, he had the legal right as feudal lord of Scotland to dispose of a rebellious subject's property; but such a claim as that would be dismissed as meaningless north of the Border. For the Percys to gain effective possession would require considerable military effort. Henry may have hoped that this would so preoccupy them that they would cease to be interested in English matters. He may also have calculated that the grant would disrupt the relationship between Hotspur and his captive, the Earl of Douglas, the man who stood to lose his patrimony.

Whatever motives lay behind the grant, Hotspur responded positively by launching an attack on Cocklaws Tower at Ormiston, a village about a mile south of Hawick and deep in Douglas territory. Clearly, he was intent on giving substance to the grant. The commander of Cocklaws garrison played by the rules by which war was conducted: having successfully resisted for long enough to satisfy honour, he agreed to surrender on 1 August, if by then the Duke of Albany had not relieved him. Peter McNiven has argued that Hotspur had bitten off more than the Percys could chew, in that without royal help they were incapable of withstanding the full weight of the Scottish state. This seems doubtful at this juncture. As Stephen Boardman has emphasised, the recent fracturing of the political scene in Scotland, together with the substantial diminution of Scottish military power by the defeats at Nisbet Muir and Humbleton Hill, meant that an effective response was beyond Albany's capability. Moreover, Murdoch, Earl of Fife, Albany's son and heir, was a prisoner, and therefore a hostage, in Henry IV's possession. Consequently, any hostile move on Albany's part would make more difficult the task of recovering his son. What the Earl and Hotspur needed was the money due to them in order to sustain their military strength: on 30 May the Earl wrote to the Council and on 26 June to the king personally (signing the letter in his own hand), asking for funds. The letters make it clear that the successful completion of the Ormiston enterprise was the urgent cause of the request.

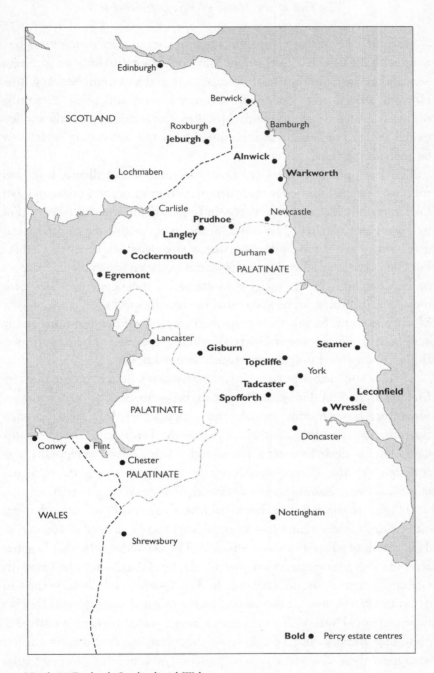

Northern England, Scotland and Wales

Hotspur's Teviotdale campaign, albeit in abeyance following his agreement with the Cocklaws garrison in May, would seem to indicate southern Scotland as the main theatre of Percy activity and ambition. Yet on 9 July, Hotspur arrived at Chester with about 200 men and began recruiting troops as a prelude to rebellion. The reasons for this apparently sudden switch are hard to fathom, but the situation in and concerning Wales may be the surest guide.

The development of the Glyn Dŵr–Mortimer–Percy alliance is hidden from us, but the knowledge that there was communication between Glyn Dŵr's court in Wales and the Percys in England indicates that some sort of plot was being hatched. The nature of that plot can only be surmised, but it is hard to avoid the conclusion that it envisaged fundamental change. For Glyn Dŵr, the adherence of the Percys would considerably increase his military strength in his struggle to create an independent Wales with himself as its prince, an outcome that he would expect the Percys and the Mortimers to ratify. For their part, the Percy–Mortimer aim must surely have been the overthrow of Henry IV and his replacement by a Mortimer, although whether by uncle or nephew is not known.

There is one further puzzle: Hotspur arrived at Chester accompanied by Archibald, Earl of Douglas. Why had he, who became a prisoner in September 1402, become an ally and supporter by July 1403? Stephen Boardman's reasonable conclusion is that the Percys and Douglas must have done a deal: in return for Douglas help, which potentially was considerable, the Percys would release prisoners, waive the Douglas ransom or even abandon their ambition to annex Douglas territory.

Douglas must also have been influenced by the knowledge that his bitter rival, George Dunbar, Earl of March, had gone over to Henry IV. This switch of adherence too is a puzzle. The answer may be that Dunbar accepted that his primary loyalty was to Henry IV, to whom he owed his safe conduct to reside in England. And he would surely have wished to desert the Percys once he was aware that the planned rebellion involved his sworn enemy, Douglas. If this is true, it suggests that Hotspur's move was no sudden impulse, but a carefully weighed decision. And this conclusion is supported by Douglas's proven presence in Edinburgh in early July, presumably gathering support for his venture with Hotspur.

With everything going their way in Scotland, the Percys must have calculated that they could afford to put their ambitions there on hold and move against Henry IV, using the combined forces of Owain Glyn Dŵr, the Earl of Douglas and their own considerable resources. They may have cynically calculated that it would be easy to reactivate their Scottish plans once they had secured a pliant government at Westminster.

As Peter McNiven and Philip Morgan have shown, Hotspur's part in the rebellion was very substantially a Cheshire affair. He had evidently used his time as Justice of Chester to establish extensive influence among the gentry and to build up a sizeable retinue: Morgan has shown that by the early summer of 1403 he had sixty-five men at arms and nearly 500 archers from the county serving with him in Scotland. Hotspur's attraction for these Cheshire men, apart from wages, may have been his military reputation with its assurance of profitable warfare; but their willingness to go beyond normal service and to join him in rebellion almost certainly stemmed from their strongly pro-Ricardian, and therefore anti-Henrician, sentiments, of which he would have been well aware. It is perhaps not surprising that, as McNiven has revealed, among the many who committed themselves to Hotspur's cause were six of the seven commanders of Richard's Cheshire bodyguard. And once in Cheshire, Hotspur attempted to boost his support by playing upon the widespread pro-Ricardian attachment by spreading rumours that Richard was still alive and would join them, together with the Earl, at Sandiway in the Delamere Forest in late August. How many were sufficiently deceived by this blatant subterfuge cannot be determined, but it is likely that it would have yielded some dividend.

But a much more valuable and certain addition to his strength was his uncle, Thomas Percy, who until that moment was at Shrewsbury with the Prince of Wales as his guardian, the role to which he had been appointed in 1402. Now, for the second time, he deserted his king in a crisis. In 1399, his reason was clear: self-preservation, added to which was that Richard's desertion of his household would mitigate any charge of disloyalty. Such a consideration is not so obvious on this second occasion, although to have been in Henry's camp when the rebellion became public would have been awkward, to say the least. The alternative and reasonable explanation is that whatever loyalty to Henry he had was dissipated by the king's treatment of him. Also, there was family solidarity: he probably felt unable to fight for a king his nephew was seeking to depose. What is unclear is the point or stage at which he was drawn into the plot. His move, however, was militarily significant in that he brought with him eight knights, 96 esquires and 866 archers, most of them staunch Ricardians and/or Cheshire men, that constituted over a quarter of the Prince's force.

What was Hotspur's stategy? The unavoidable conclusion must be that his primary objective was Shrewsbury, in order to capture the Prince of Wales and eliminate his retinue, now probably reduced to about 2,500 men. Also, with the prince in his hands, potentially he had the means of forcing concessions from the king. This would have been the more timid and uncertain policy and unlikely to succeed. Any concessions the king might make to secure the release of his heir could immediately be withdrawn as being made under duress, leaving Hotspur and his uncle completely vulnerable. Moreover, the prospect of a Mortimer succession would have vanished. Bolder and more drastic would have been to murder the young Henry, which would provoke a decisive battle with his father, with victory opening the way to the Mortimer succession.

Possession of Shrewsbury was also a military imperative in that it would have given him control of one of the main crossings of the Severn, and so enable him to effect a link-up with Glyn Dŵr. It has to be said, however, that there is no definite proof that this was the plan. At that moment Glyn Dŵr was apparently trying to extend his control into South Wales, that is, he was moving away from, not towards, Hotspur. However, this does not necessarily invalidate the notion that the two men were working to an agreed plan.

Whatever Hotspur's plans were, they were frustrated by the speed of Henry IV's reaction. He was already on the move north, reaching Nottingham on 12 July, when he was informed of what was happening. He immediately altered course and headed westwards through Derby to Burton upon Trent and Lichfield, where he halted from 16 to 19 July in order to write to Hotspur requesting a meeting, but also to the sheriffs of sixteen counties ordering the muster of troops. Meanwhile, on the 17th

Hotspur was at Sandiway to meet the men who had turned out in his (or Richard II's) cause. The crucial point of these movements was that it was Henry who got to Shrewsbury before Hotspur. In doing so, he secured the services of around 2,500 seasoned troops, prevented his son becoming a hostage or worse and placed himself between Hotspur and Glyn Dŵr. Hotspur was now on the back foot. Resolution by battle was now avoidable only by capitulation, a reaction not in Hotspur's nature.

The battle was fought on Saturday 21 July. As with almost all medieval battles, the exact site is a matter of dispute. This should not be so in this case, since a chantry church with a college, comprising a master and seven chaplains, to intercede for the souls of those killed was founded in 1409 and 1410 (with Henry IV providing most of the endowment) on the supposed site of the battle. However, alternative locations nearby have been proposed. One is that Hotspur drew up his army along a ridge a little to the north of the church, while a more recent study argues that a number of fields in the village of Harlesey, someway south of the church, fit more closely the description of where the fighting took place. There is also a local tradition that places the site of Hotspur's death west of the church. While it would be satisfying to be able to identify the exact whereabouts of the battle site, and archaeology may yet reveal this, it is certain that it was in the vicinity of the church, which still stands.

As regards the two armies, it is fairly certain that the king's was somewhat larger. But actual sizes are impossible to determine, although given that both were assembled in a hurry, it is probably safer to go for lower rather than higher figures. With all that we know of army sizes in the late fourteenth century, it seems unlikely that Henry's force would have exceeded 8,000 men, with Hotspur having around 5,000. The fighting was preceded, as was common, by conference, the aim of which was to see if battle could be avoided. The king's representatives were the Abbots of Shrewsbury and Haughmond, the latter's house being within sight of the two armies, while Hotspur sent his uncle, Thomas Percy, Earl of Worcester, despite the fact that Henry had requested a personal interview. The story that Thomas used his role to exacerbate the differences instead of trying to bring about a peaceful out come, is hard to credit. More credible is that George Dunbar urged Henry to fight that day, while he had numerical superiority, pointing out that delay would give Hotspur time to augment his army.

The course of medieval battles is notoriously difficult to determine, and so it is with Shrewsbury. What is known is that it began with an archery duel, in which Hotspur's men appear to have made the greater impact, not surprisingly, if many of them were veterans of the Ricardian bodyguard. But this was not decisive, and the battle degenerated into a hand-to-hand melée. It seems clear that Hotspur's aim was to kill the king, which would eliminate need for a post-victory judicial murder. On the other side, Dunbar, aware of the danger, persuaded Henry to withdraw from the fighting, leaving two decoy look-alikes. The ruse worked: both were slain, but Henry was not. Had he been killed, the battle would have been over, bar the pursuit. Instead, it was Hotspur who died. How is not known for certain; it may have been by an arrow in the face as he raised his visor. As the news spread, the fight became pointless for the rebels and the rout began. The event had lasted between two and three hours and was a savage and bloody affair. The number of dead buried on the battlefield was variously estimated at 1,500, 1,847 and 2,291 and there were other burial pits within a three-mile radius.

And the bloodletting was not over. Hotspur's body was recovered and buried at Whitchurch by Lord Furnival, a member of the king's army. This was an act of familial piety since Thomas Neville, Lord Furnival was a cousin of the Earl. Hotspur was not allowed to rest in peace, at least at this juncture. His body was exhumed and, as was customary with those deemed guilty of treason, quartered, the four parts being sent for display to Newcastle, London, Chester and Bristol, and the head to York. The indignity was not protracted. Once the need for public awareness had been satisfied, the parts were returned to Hotspur's wife, Elizabeth, in November for burial in York Minster. Hotspur's fate was more merciful than that of his uncle, Thomas Percy, who was captured after the battle. Together with two leading Cheshire knights, Sir Richard Vernon and Sir Richard Venables, he was hung, drawn and quartered as a traitor the following day. It is said that Henry was inclined to spare him, but was talked out of doing so by his close advisers.

The leading question about the Battle of Shrewsbury, as at Otterburn, is the Earl's absence. If he was fully involved in his son's scheme, and it is not certain that he was, the most plausible explanation is that he was prevented from joining his son by superior forces assembled in Yorkshire. The man blocking his path was Ralph Neville, Earl of Westmorland, whose ability to raise a large body of troops was demonstrated in the Scottish campaign of 1400. With him was one of Henry's most trusted aides, Sir Robert Waterton, who may have been in Yorkshire to mobilise the Lancastrian affinity, which was numerous in the county. He may also have had additional support from Lord Willoughby, to whom he was related by marriage, and from his friend Sir Ralph Eure.

This may explain why the Earl chose not to fight but to retreat into Northumberland. He requested admission to Newcastle, but the town authorities were prepared to allow only the Earl himself and his personal attendants, not his troops, to enter the town. Consequently, he retreated further north to his castle at Warkworth. The date of the Earl's decision is also important. One account says that the Earl was turned back before the battle, while another gives the date as 30 July, when he would probably have known the outcome of the battle. If the former date is correct, the notion of superior military strength under Westmorland's command would appear to be valid. But if the latter is correct, the Earl probably decided that the game was up and that to press on would be suicidal. But it is also possible that the Earl may have deliberately moved in a dilatory fashion out of another consideration. He may have decided upon a fail-safe strategy in the hope of preserving his family from total disaster should Hotspur's venture fail.

If this was his aim, he was successful. On 11 August, he met Henry at York, having been given an assurance that he would not be harmed and that he would be allowed to defend himself before Parliament. There, he claimed that Hotspur had acted without his approval, but he agreed to hand over his castles to the king and to relinquish his public offices. Pending the meeting of Parliament, he was held as a prisoner, first at Pontefract, and then at Baginton Castle, near Coventry. Henry bestowed the offices of Constable and Warden of the East March on his third son, John, now fourteen years old. He gave the West March to Ralph Neville, Earl of Westmorland, but as he was also Prince John's tutor, the effect was to replace Percy with Neville as the supreme authority in the Border zone.

The process of dealing with the Earl's offence took place in the Parliament that met between January and March 1404. Precisely what happened is not clear, but there appears to have been an inclination on the part of both the king and the Lords and Commons to avoid finding the Earl guilty of treason. Instead, he was convicted of the much more minor offence of 'trespass'. Afterwards, he renewed his fealty to the king, who excused his fine. He had been treated very leniently.

But leniency was the hallmark of Henry's reactions to the Percys throughout the uprising. He appears to have been genuinely puzzled by Hotspur's rebellion and at some pains to resolve his grievances by negotiation, to allow Thomas Percy his life and in the end to allow the Earl to escape with the lightest of punishments. Henry may not have felt politically strong enough to take a harsh line against such a powerful and well-entrenched magnate, particularly in the face of what seems to have been parliamentary inclination towards giving him the benefit of the doubt. Evidence of the depth of loyalty the Earl commanded, and of the qualified nature of his submission, was clearly revealed in the refusal of the commanders of the Earl's garrisons at Berwick, Alnwick and Warkworth to obey the royal mandate to hand over their castles to the king's officials. At the same time, Henry may have recognised that if he needed Neville to balance Percy, he also needed Percy to balance Neville: to prevent serious or complete loss of Crown control in the Border zone, it was essential to prevent one family acquiring entrenched power. His decision to place his son in a titular role, which could become increasingly active as Prince John approached manhood, may indicate a long-term aim of increasing the Crown's direct involvement in the affairs of the Border zone, as it was clear he aimed to do in Wales.

Rebellion, 1405

The Earl recovered his estates in the course of 1404 and by the end of the year he was again attending the meetings of the Council. His prospects, however, were not good. Conceivably, by a display of exemplary behaviour, he might have regained one of the wardenships, although any hope of dislodging the Nevilles would have been unrealistic. But he chose not to follow this course. Instead, in the late spring of the following year he was again in rebellion against Henry IV, with the aim, it must be assumed, of overthrowing the Lancastrian regime.

Perhaps the clearest evidence that this was so is the compact, known as the Tripartite Indenture, he made with Glyn Dŵr and Sir Edmund Mortimer that was sealed, probably at Bangor in North Wales and probably on 28 February 1405. By its terms, the three parties swore to defend the realm of England against all men, suggesting that they were committed to maintain the integrity of the kingdom. But in one of the clauses, in which they laid down their respective spheres of power, they proposed to redraw its political geography in such a way as to dismember it. Glyn Dŵr was to have the whole of Wales plus the parts of England to the west of a line drawn from Worcester to the source of the Trent, thence to the source of the Mersey and then along that river to the sea. This line completely ignored ancient English county boundaries so that all of Cheshire, Hereford and Shropshire but only the western parts of Worcestershire, Gloucestershire and Staffordshire were to be incorporated into an enlarged Wales. The Percy share was also to be an enlargement of their traditional area of dominance: the northern counties plus the counties of Derby, Nottingham, Lincoln, Leicester, Warwick, Northampton and Norfolk. Not included were Cumberland and Durham. The omission of the former may have been an oversight, but Durham may have been subsumed under Northumberland, although it may equally have been an acknowledgement of the unique status of the bishop's palatinate. The remainder of England was allocated to the Mortimers.

The initiative for this scheme appears to have come from the Earl, but the phrasing of the record highlights the influence of the Welsh bards at Glyn Dŵr's court and their belief in ancient prophesies about the future division of Britain. On the other hand, it is not inconceivable that the partition proposed in 1405 was in some way a restatement of the agreement between Hotspur, Glyn Dŵr and Mortimer in 1403. How realistic the parties thought this proposed partition was, is not clear. While it may seem to us so improbable as to be bizarre, we should remember the numerous and arbitrary redrawing of boundaries that have taken place in Europe throughout its history, including our own day. And frontiers were not then, as they now tend to be, regarded as the immutable defining boundaries of nations. Rather, they were seen more as delineating the areas within which men gave, or were required to give, their allegiance to a particular ruler. Modern notions of national territory, while not absent, were less developed and not paramount. As proof of this, the numerous instances of land and allegiance transfers and attempted transfers that took place in the fourteenth and fifteenth centuries, including the efforts of English kings to acquire parts of France and Scotland, may be cited.

But why did the Earl reactivate the Glyn Dŵr alliance? The answer almost certainly lies in the situation in Wales. As Rees Davies has shown, in the course of 1404, Glyn Dŵr made considerable progress in his campaign to become master of all of Wales. During that year, he captured the important castles of Harlech and Aberystwyth and gained control of Glamorgan. His power had become sufficiently extensive and apparently certain for him to seek and gain in July 1404 an alliance with the French government, which in August 1405 sent a small army to help him. At this stage, probably correctly, the French government saw the Welsh as a more useful ally than the Scots. In addition, he had in his hands the senior member of the house of Mortimer, whose claim to the throne of England was bound up with those of the Percys.

That the Mortimers were considered vital to the scheme is underlined by the attempt in mid-February, that is, just before the Tripartite Indenture was sealed, by Constance, widow of Thomas, Lord Despenser (executed in 1400) to abduct the young Earl of March and his brother from Windsor Castle, where she and her son were also in residence. Initially, the attempt was successful, Lady Despenser and the three boys managing to escape from the castle with a considerable sum of money. However, the party was overtaken and captured at Cheltenham. The westward direction of their flight clearly points to their intention of preventing the murder of the young Mortimers by Henry IV and reuniting them with their uncle at Glyn Dŵr's court. Moreover, that this attempt was made while the partition scheme was being concocted can leave little doubt that it was an integral element in the planning of a co-ordinated rebellion.

But the rebellion that broke out in May 1405 occurred in Yorkshire. In fact there were two uprisings, one in the North Riding, led by members of the gentry; the other by Richard Scrope, Archbishop of York, third son of Henry, Lord Scrope of Masham, who had had a conventional clerical career and had up to this point never evinced any strong political leanings. With him was Thomas Mowbray, the nineteen-year-old heir of Thomas Mowbray, Earl of Nottingham and Duke of Norfolk, who had been exiled by Richard II in 1398 and had died abroad. Given that his father's exile was the consequence of his quarrel with the then Henry of Bolingbroke, young Mowbray's animosity against the king is understandable.

Scrope's reasons were set out in a manifesto, either written or approved by him, copies of which were nailed to church doors in York. The grievances listed, which encompassed all sectors of society, were expressed in very general terms, so making them hard to interpret. They begin to make sense, however, in the light of the current European trade situation and the radical solutions proposed by the Commons in the Parliament held at Coventry in October 1404. The most drastic was that the clergy should hand over their temporalities to the Crown as a temporary measure. This came to nothing, due to the fiercely argued opposition of the Archbishop of Canterbury, Thomas Arundel; but that it was actually proposed must have raised considerable anxiety in all the clergy, including Scrope, who had the responsibility to defend his own interests and those of the clergy of his archdiocese. The Commons were more successful with their demand that all grants of Crown land made since 1366 should be revoked. The king agreed to this in principle, but stalled for time by successfully arguing that it could not be fairly implemented until a survey to identify accurately what were Crown lands had reported. As a stopgap, the Commons voted that all holders of annuities, sinecures and grants for profit made under letters patent should forgo their current year's income. The Commons was sufficiently convinced that they would get action that they not only voted two-tenths and two-fifteenths, but they proposed a number of novel taxes: 1s (5p) in every pound from land rents; 20s (100p) in every £20 from land valued at over 500 marks (£333.34) per annum; and a tax on chattels of 1s (5p) from those worth £20 and 2s (10p) from those worth £40. These measures clearly affected every stratum of landowning society. As regards the merchant community, it was concerned by the growing trade war with the Hanseatic cities of North Germany that culminated in their imposing a trade embargo with England in March 1405.

Were these Yorkshire uprisings separate enterprises, independent of the Glyn Dŵr–Mortimer–Percy conspiracy, and, if not, how were they connected? After a detailed examination of the evidence, Peter McNiven concluded that the Earl and Scrope were in collusion, although coming to rebellion from very different starting points: Scrope aimed to secure reform of government; the Earl aimed to control it. Scrope's programme, McNiven believes, gave the Earl a veneer of respectability. But recently, Simon Walker has challenged this, arguing that there were three distinct events, only one of which involved the Earl. This was his attempt with 400 of his retinue to seize the Earl of Westmorland while he was staying with Sir Ralph Eure, one of his close associates, at Eure's castle at Witton le Wear in Durham. This, he believes, was the first move that would have opened the way to an unopposed advance south into Yorkshire, where the Earl could expect substantially to augment his force from his tenantry and the many gentry accustomed to follow the Percy lead. His plans beyond that point are conjectural, although pressing on to join his allies in the west would have been a logical move. But, Westmorland got wind of the Earl's intention and, having escaped to the safety of Durham Castle, informed the king, who sent his Master of Horse, Robert Waterton, to find out what was happening. The Earl clarified the situation by arresting and detaining the royal emissary.

Walker also sees the two Yorkshire uprisings as separate events. That by the citizenry of York answered the call of the Archbishop; the other, by men from Cleveland and around Topcliffe, was the work of four North Yorkshire knights: Ralph Hastings, John Fauconberg, John Fitzrandolph and John Colville, and the Priors of Warter and Old Malton, who had their own discontents. All of them, however, had long association with the Percys adherents; consequently, although Walker's view that Scrope acted independently of the Earl may be correct, it is hard not to believe that the North Riding gentry were not acting in conjunction with and in response to the Earl's wishes and in preparation for his arrival. If Walker has weakened

McNiven's idea of a single movement, he may have pushed his own argument too far. Again, it may be safest to recognise that, although the main outline of events is not in dispute, motives and linkages cannot be determined with complete certainty.

Initially, Westmorland seems to have planned to remain in Durham so as to block any southward move by the Earl. But he was then joined by the Northumberland knight, Sir Robert Umfraville, who was aware that following his failure at Witton le Wear the Earl had aborted his plan and had headed north and that therefore it was safe for Westmorland to advance into Yorkshire. Were he to act quickly, he had a good chance of preventing the Cleveland rebels joining forces with those from York and its vicinity, who were already encamped on Shipton Moor, six miles north-west of the city.

Westmorland took the advice, and by 27 May he, together with Umfraville, Sir Ralph Eure and Sir Henry Fitzhugh with their retinues, got to Shipton Moor before the Cleveland rebels arrived. For three days there was a stand-off, but on 29 May Neville brought the rebellion to an end by trickery. He invited Scrope and the other rebel leaders to bring their demands to him. On reading them he declared that they were entirely reasonable and that he would willingly plead their case with the king. This being his promise, he suggested that the rebel leaders should dismiss their troops, as their presence no longer served any useful purpose. As soon as this had been done, he promptly arrested Scrope and his associates and hurried them off to Pontefract Castle. The king arrived there a week later, and from there moved to the Archbishop's manor at Bishopthorpe. Two days later, on 8 June at Clementhorpe, outside the city, the leaders of the rebellion were executed as traitors. The death of Mowbray was to be expected, but the execution of the archbishop was unprecedented and was carried out despite the plea of the Archbishop of Canterbury, who interceded with the king for the life of his fellow metropolitan. Also, the Chief Justice of the King's Bench, Sir William Gascoigne, resigned on the ground that for him to be party to this act would be acting *ultra vires*.

The Earl's retreat north can be explained, not only by his failure at Witton le Wear, but also by his failure to bring to his side men like Umfraville, Eure and Fitzhugh, men of substance with considerable retinues. As Andy King has shown, while these leading members of the Northumberland community were willing to accept the Earl's leadership in Border matters, they were not prepared to follow, and could not be coerced into following, him into rebellion. And he may have known or suspected that the king was advancing north with an army. The Earl managed to trick his way into Berwick, where he entered into negotiations with the Scottish government, offering surrender of Berwick in return for help, and also through them with the Duke of Orleans in France. He remained there until the approach of the king, who in the second half of June advanced steadily northwards, securing the surrender of the Earl's castles. As nothing came of his diplomatic efforts, the Earl fled from Berwick into Scotland. He did so under the protection of Sir David Fleming and Henry Sinclair, Earl of Orkney, the chief supporters of Robert III, who in the aftermath of Humbleton Hill had resumed an active political role. Berwick immediately opened its gates upon Henry's arrival, and, by 12 July, the castle surrendered to him after a brief artillery bombardment. At least eight of its garrison were executed, which encouraged the prompt surrender of Alnwick Castle by Sir William Clifford and Sir Henry Percy of Atholl, the Earl's grandson.

The Earl's decision not to fight after his failure to capture Westmorland may have been panic, but the more likely reason is that he recognised that he had failed to secure enough support to continue. He also had another and very urgent consideration, namely the safety of his grandson, Henry Percy, Hotspur's son. After the 1403 failure, the Earl had taken the precaution of sending the boy to Scotland for safekeeping. It is a measure of the Earl's political importance that Robert III lodged the Earl's grandson with his own heir, James, whom he placed in the care of the Bishop of St Andrews, Henry Wardlaw. The Earl's decision to leave his heir there once he had made his peace with Henry IV may be further evidence of his intention to rebel again. In ducking the challenge after his failure at Witton le Wear, he may have been more concerned for the safety of his grandson than for himself and the rebellion with its diminished chances of success. He was now sixty-three, while his grandson was only in his twelfth year. This boy, Hotspur's son, was the family's future, and needed protection until he became an adult. After the Earl's death, hopefully, the young Henry Percy would be able to restore the Percy fortunes and benefit from the Mortimer connection.

Rebellion, 1408

The Earl's flight made his treason patent. The related processes, however, were slow. It was not until June 1406 that he was formally summoned to answer the charge of treason. His failure to appear resulted in the forfeiture of his titles and estates. Later in the year, he was tried by the Court of Chivalry and then attainted by Parliament. Meanwhile, his estates were used to reward loyalists and to provide endowments for the queen and Prince John. In disposing of the Percy lands, Henry was careful to grant them for life, not in perpetuity: the recipients got the loan, not the ownership. This may have been the consequence of Henry's determination to increase Crown control in the Border zone. On the other hand, by this date the nobility had become hostile to the notion that the Crown was free to destroy a family: the king had the right to crush a rebel or a traitor, but he was not expected to visit that man's sins upon his innocent descendants. Henry IV, above all men, was aware of how important it was to handle this sort of situation circumspectly and with an eye to the future.

Henry's other response was to release the Earl of Douglas on parole with a commission to negotiate an exchange of prisoners: himself and Murdoch Stewart, Earl of Fife for the Earl and Lord Bardolf, the Earl's chief supporter in the rebellion. While Robert III was alive this was unlikely to happen. But by 1406 his health was failing, and his mistrust of his brother, Robert Stewart, Duke of Albany, led him to place James on the Bass Rock for safety in the custody of Sir David Fleming. But on 14 February, the murder of Fleming by Sir James Douglas, the Earl of Douglas's younger brother, led to the decision that James would only be safe in France. The move misfired: on 14 March, the ship on which James was travelling was captured off Flamborough Head by an English vessel; the boy who would shortly become King of Scots entered captivity in England that would last eighteen years. In fact, it was the news of his son's fate that precipitated Robert III's death on 4 April.

151

Albany now became regent. His prime concern, however, was the recovery of his son, not his nephew, and in this the Earl would have been an excellent bargaining counter. But the Earl was no longer in Scotland. Tipped off as to his likely fate, he fled Scotland and sought refuge in Wales, accompanied by Lord Bardolf and two Welsh bishops, Lewis Byford of Bangor and John Trefor of St Asaph.

The Earl clearly hoped again to revive the alliance with Glyn Dŵr, although he would now be the junior partner. This move might have brought success had not Glyn Dŵr's fortunes been in decline. The English government's tactic of slow attrition was yielding results. Glyn Dŵr lost several members of his family, killed or captured; the small but vital French army returned home; and some Welsh landowners deserted his cause and made peace with the government. Then in April and June 1406, he suffered two serious military defeats. In the first, the Welsh suffered very heavy casualties; and in the second, a force commanded by the Earl and Lord Bardolf was routed by Edward Charlton, Lord Powys. Sometime after this episode, the Earl left Wales for France.

There he had grounds for hoping that he would get support. In 1404, the death of Philippe the Bold, Duke of Burgundy, opened the way for Louis II, Duke of Orleans to gain control of the French government. Orleans' policy was anti-English, hence his active support for Glyn Dŵr's rebellion and his decision to betroth his son, Charles, to Isabelle, the widow of Richard II. His days of undisputed power were short-lived, however, as he was successfully challenged by the new Duke of Burgundy, Philippe the Bold's son, Jean, known as 'the Fearless'. The consequence was that the Earl's petition to the French royal council for help in deposing Henry IV and putting Edmund Mortimer on the throne was rejected. How long the Earl stayed in France is not clear, but at some stage he moved to Flanders, although why is uncertain. What is known is that he and his companions returned to Scotland some time in the summer of 1407.

It was therefore in the later months of the year that the Earl must have resolved to try once more to take on Henry IV by launching an invasion of England. This was probably desperate necessity: simply, he had no alternative as he had run out of safe havens and possible backers. For certain, Scotland under Albany, whose son was still captive in England, was a doubtful refuge. Knowing that reconciliation with Henry IV was out of the question, his best hope was that discontent in England was sufficient to win him the necessary support. It was a high-risk gamble, but such a gamble had paid off in 1399. Reports of his agents, however, were negative and he must therefore have known that a repeat of 1399 was unlikely. But, rather than be tamely delivered by Albany to Henry IV for certain execution, he opted for another trial of strength. His situation was desperate, hence his decision to launch an ill-equipped campaign in mid-winter.

Even here, he had no luck: the winter of 1407–8 proved to be the worst in living memory, with snow persisting from December until March, just the conditions to encourage men to stay at home. The size of his following cannot have been large, and may have included a number of adventurous Scots in addition to his own people. He appears to have gained few recruits in Northumberland, although he was joined by the Prior of Hexham; likewise in Durham, where the new bishop, Thomas Langley, was a committed Lancastrian, and the Earl of Westmorland dominated lay society. In Yorkshire, however, men came in from the Percy estates in the North Riding. But they appear to have been from rural society and not to have included any of the knights and esquires who traditionally answered the Percy call.

News of the invasion brought the Sheriff of Yorkshire, Sir Thomas Rokeby, into action. With what too was a small force, he prevented the Earl crossing the River Nidd near Knaresborough. However, the Earl managed to get across lower downstream and then to occupy a defensive position on Bramham Moor, about four miles south of Wetherby. There, on Sunday 19 February 1408, Rokeby attacked him with a force that may have been smaller in size but was probably better equipped for battle. The Earl died in the brief time the conflict lasted. Bardolf was captured, but died of his wounds, while the remainder of the Earl's little army fled or were captured. The Earl's body was submitted to the traditional indignity of being quartered, the four parts of the torso being exposed at Newcastle, Berwick, York and Lincoln, while the head was sent to London. This ritual humiliation lasted until July, when the parts were reunited for burial beside the grave of his son, Hotspur, at the right side of the high altar of York Minster. His nemesis, Rokeby, was duly rewarded with a grant for life of Spofforth, one of the largest Percy manors in Yorkshire.

Conclusion and Postscript

Death and Resurrection, 1408–85

The failure of the Percy family to depose the man they had put on the throne should not be regarded as inevitable. Henry IV appears never to have been fully certain in his own mind about the legitimacy of his title, and the continuing rumours that Richard II was still alive told him that many people were of the same opinion. Shakespeare was right to put into his mouth the words 'uneasy lies the head that wears the crown', certainly one obtained in the circumstances of 1399. Not only did he fear rebellion, but it is likely that he had a sense of moral unease, knowing himself to be a perjured usurper.

Arguably, the Percys were correct in considering that Edmund Mortimer's right to the throne had greater validity than that of Henry of Bolingbroke. Their conviction, however, had nothing to do with righteousness, but everything to do with self-interest. Their failure to press Mortimer's case in 1399, and there is no convincing evidence that they did, denies them any claim to the upper moral ground of legal or constitutional correctness. What made the Mortimer claim attractive was Hotspur's marriage to Elizabeth Mortimer and, assuming Edmund Mortimer became king, the consequent proximity of their son, Henry, to the throne. Although this prospect existed in 1399, it was so hypothetical that it was not worth the sacrifice of the very gains that were to be had from supporting Bolingbroke. By 1403, however, the situation was changed in two respects. Bolingbroke as Henry IV had failed, and intentionally so, to be the king the Percys wanted. More positively, the success of Owain Glyn Dŵr's rebellion and his alliance with Sir Edmund Mortimer provided the Percys with the support they needed. By themselves, the Percys probably did not have the power to topple Henry IV, but in alliance with Glyn Dŵr their chances of doing so were realistic.

155

Why did they fail? The prime reason is that at the crucial moments they were too slow to act and Henry IV was too quick for them. This was most clearly demonstrated in 1403, the occasion when their chance of success was greatest, by the speed with which Henry got to Shrewsbury. Once he was there, Hotspur's initial advantage of surprise disappeared. The second factor in 1403 was the failure of the three parties to coalesce: had they done so, Henry would have found it hard to withstand them. It therefore remains something of a mystery why this did not happen, especially why the Earl was apparently so dilatory. The third factor undoubtedly was the commitment of Ralph Neville, Earl of Westmorland. If, as has been argued, Henry created what in effect was a Beaufort party in the early 1400s, to which Westmorland was attached by marriage, it served him well. In both 1403 and 1405, it was the prompt action by Neville that was a vital ingredient in Henry's success. In 1403, Neville prevented the junction of the Earl and his son; and in 1405, he prevented the Earl joining forces with Archbishop Scrope, and by his guile snuffed out the latter's threat. Thanks to him, the principle of 'divide and conquer' was successfully applied on both occasions. In both 1403 and 1405, the Percys had a real chance of winning their gamble. In 1408, they did not. The Earl's invasion was the futile gesture of a man near the end of his days, for whom there was probably not even the alternative of a quiet and ignominious passing in a foreign land. At least by making the attempt he met, in the terms of the *mores* of his class, an honourable death.

How should the Percys be assessed? This is no easy task and all comments must be hedged about with qualifications. Perhaps the best starting point is James Sherborne's conclusion that 'the Percies are hard men to fathom'. The most able appears to have been Thomas Percy, who, as a younger son, had to make his own way in the world, albeit with the help of an illustrious name. He was clearly an able soldier, and perhaps a more able fighting sailor, who appears to have enjoyed his military days in Iberia, France and the Channel. He was also a very competent diplomat, as is witnessed by the many missions in which he took part or led on behalf of both the two kings he served, and also John of Gaunt. These wide-ranging abilities and experiences made his support worth having, a fact that

Richard II recognised in appointing him to the top posts in his household in the 1390s.

At crucial moments, however, Thomas broke faith and betrayed trust. In doing so he committed the cardinal sin of chivalric society. On both occasions, it can be argued that the urgent needs of his family outweighed loyalty to his master. This is perhaps not clear-cut in 1399, when his decision to disband Richard II's household was taken at the moment when the royal cause must have seemed doomed and when Richard may have fled without informing his Steward. This said, his immediate move to join Bolingbroke and his brother and nephew ensured that there was some validity in the charge of betrayal. The significance of Thomas Percy's act should not be underestimated: by it, he deprived Richard of the main engine of royal power and publicly signalled that Richard's reign was effectively at an end. Moreover, his actions ensured that there was no ambiguity in the Percy family's attitude to the imminent change of regime, which in turn would strengthen their hand in their dealings with the future king. In 1403, however, there is little room for doubt: family loyalty was the deciding factor. His decision to desert may have been easier for him than it had been in 1399, since he probably felt closer to Richard II than he did to Henry IV, who, in removing him as Steward of the Household, put Percy's importance and value to him in true perspective.

If Thomas was the ablest of the Percys, Hotspur was the most glamorous in the minds of contemporaries and, thanks to Shakespeare's flawed portrait, to our own time. As far as I am aware, no other medieval hero has given his name to a boys' adventure magazine and a leading football club. To men and women of his day, he exemplified to a high degree the expected qualities of the knight: brave and dashing, the complete warrior, and moreover chivalrous. This last point deserves emphasis, since mere military prowess would have been insufficient to give him the reputation he enjoyed. This aspect of his character is illustrated by the incident in 1402, when he came to court from Wales to report on his negotiations with Glyn Dŵr. There, its less military active members upbraided him for not using the opportunity to seize Glyn Dŵr, whom he met under safe conduct, on the ground that the Welshman was a declared traitor. Hotspur was so outraged by the notion that he should have broken his given word that he stormed out of the meeting. This stands in contrast to the deceit practised upon Scrope by Ralph Neville at Shipton Moor; and it may help to explain why in the end Neville was a success and Hotspur a failure.

On that occasion, Hotspur is said to have contrasted his life in the field with that of the inactive courtiers. And this reminds us that Hotspur was first and last a military man, although, in terms of battles won, not a notably successful one. He fought three major set-piece battles: Otterburn, Humbleton Hill and Shrewsbury. The first he lost, largely through his rush to fight in the gloaming after a forced march. What would have happened had he chosen to pause and allowed his troops to recover from their march and the Bishop of Durham to catch up with him with additional men is an interesting but inadmissible question. What can be said is that the impetuosity that gave him his sobriquet was a major reason for his defeat. Humbleton Hill, the battle that avenged Otterburn, was a victory, but one due less to Hotspur's generalship than to the tactical acumen of George Dunbar in persuading Hotspur that the archers, not the men at arms, were the key to victory. His final battle at Shrewsbury, it may be argued, was lost before it began, once he had failed to get into the town and seize the Prince of Wales before the king arrived. Thereafter, he had to fight with the disadvantage of a smaller army. In the circumstances, his tactic of a charge into the fray in an attempt to kill the king was probably right, but again George Dunbar, with his advocacy of decoy 'kings', was the shrewder general. Hotspur's reputation as a warrior is justified, but he does not get high marks as a commander. The camp appears to have been Hotspur's natural home. Unlike both his father and his uncle, there is no record of his being used in diplomacy and he was not much involved in, and perhaps not entirely at ease with, the two-faced world of politics.

This does not mean that he was without ambition. The very fact that he took the lead in the 1403 rebellion is sufficient evidence of serious aims. What precisely they were, however, is not absolutely clear. Certainly he was at one with his father in wanting to secure permanent control over the Border zone; but it is possible that his ambitions extended beyond this region. A further motivating force was the knowledge of his son's royal ancestry. It would be going too far to argue that he aimed to make him king, but he was aware that if Edmund Mortimer were to become king, then his son had a chance, however slight, of succeeding him. While Henry IV was king, this was an impossible dream. The circumstances of 1403 made the temptation too attractive to resist.

The Earl is the most difficult of the three Percys to assess. During the early part of his career he appears to have been at least competent as a soldier, but after he became Earl his appetite for war seems to have declined, as is indicated by his poor handling of the 1384 Berwick incident: not only did his laxness allow the Scots to seize the castle, but his military action to recapture it failed, and he had to resort to bribery (2,000 marks [£1,333.34] of his own money) to induce them to surrender it and return home unmolested. It is possible that the memory of this humiliation drove Hotspur to action in August 1388.

This apparent military lassitude was again evident in the crises of the first decade of the fifteenth century when his military performance was lack-lustre. His readiness to back off when faced by Ralph Neville in 1403 and 1405 make him seem cold footed or even pusillanimous. On both occasions, his failure to strike a blow was certainly a major factor in ensuring defeat for his cause. Given his early career as a soldier, it is hard to accuse him of cowardice or timidity. It may be, of course, that in both 1403 and 1405 the force mustered by Neville was so large that to have risked battle would have been foolhardy. And in both years he may have calculated that discretion was more important than valour, especially because, as the head of his house, he had the responsibility of ensuring its survival. Nor should it be forgotten that at this time he was in his early sixties, that is to say, he was a man of very advanced years, whose health may have been poor and faculties impaired. As regards his final throw in 1408, it seems clear that it had virtually no chance of success and that the Earl may well have known this as he set out.

But in his early years he had considerable success in advancing the fortunes of his house. The award of an earldom was a significant social enhancement, which he probably owed in large measure to his association with John of Gaunt, then at the height of his influence. And the properties he acquired through his second marriage made him a major force in Cumberland and increased his power in Northumberland. It is probable that it was these successes that fuelled his ambition to become the permanent dominating authority in the Border zone, for it was this that seems to have been his aim during the rest of his life. Both the substance and the symbol of this domination was the permanent occupation of the offices of Warden of the East and West Marches. These being in the gift of the Crown, it was necessary to have sufficient influence in government to see that either he or a member of his family was appointed to both of them. This proved elusive under Richard II, hence his willingness to remove him and to have Bolingbroke as Henry IV in his place. Had this produced the desired result, it seems unlikely that the Earl would have been interested in rebellion, but it was Henry's reversion to Richard II's 'divide and rule' policy that made him realise that the new king was, from his standpoint, no better than the old. To what extent he shared any regal hopes for his grandson that Hotspur may have harboured is impossible to say, but it may have been that father and son were not fully of a mind over this, the Earl having a more realistic assessment of the possibilities.

The postscript is a study in irony. Roger Mortimer, the younger of the two sons of the Fourth Earl of March, was a sickly child who died in 1409. His elder brother, Edmund Mortimer, Fifth Earl of March, lived a normal life until the age of thirty-four, when he died of plague in January 1425. Eleven months earlier, he had married Anne, daughter of the Earl of Stafford, but their marriage produced no children. These early deaths and failures to produce offspring underline how right Hotspur had been to nurture his son's prospects. Following the Fifth Earl of March's death, the heir to the Mortimer claim was his sister, Anne, the wife of Richard, Earl of Cambridge, the younger son of Edmund of Langley, Duke of York, the fourth son of Edward III. Cambridge was executed in 1415 for his part in the plot to assassinate Henry V on the eve of his invasion of France. Thereafter, the claim devolved upon their son, Richard, Duke of York, and after his death at the Battle of Wakefield in 1460, to his son Edward, known as Earl of March. The following year, as the result of his victory over King Henry VI at Towton Moor, March became King Edward IV. In the end, therefore, the Mortimer claim to the throne triumphed.

Although Hotspur's dreams, if such they were, came to nothing, for his family there was life after death. Resurrection began in 1413 with the death of Henry IV and the accession of his son as Henry V. The new king saw the advantage to be gained by restoring many of the families slighted by his father as he prepared his attempt to gain the French throne. For the Percys this meant the release of Hotspur's son, Henry Percy, from Scotland, where since 1404 he had been a prisoner or hostage in all but name. The timing was judicious: on 3 February 1414, the year following Henry V's accession, Henry Percy reached his majority. Consequently, on 11 November 1414 formal approval was given for his return to England. But it was not until February 1416 that he actually crossed the Tweed. The reason for the delay was the complicated and lengthy negotiations needed to secure the complementary release of Murdoch, Earl of Fife, who had remained a prisoner in England since his capture by the Percys at Humbleton Hill in 1402. One strand in the arrangement was Henry Percy's marriage to Eleanor, the widow of Richard Despenser. The real significance of this was Eleanor's parentage: she was the daughter of Ralph Neville, Earl of Westmorland. Henry V's purpose was to restore the Percys to their role in Border defence, a matter made urgent by his awarenes that with him and his army in France the northern border would be vulnerable, while at the same time trying to prevent renewed Neville–Percy rivalry.

A month after his return, on 16 March 1416, Henry Percy was granted the title of Earl of Northumberland. Although the wording of the 1416 charter was identical to that of 1377, in strict terms this was a new creation, but conventionally he is regarded as the Second Earl of Northumberland. Finally, he was given permission to attempt to recover his estates, in that he was granted the right to sue in the Court of Chancery for his grandfather's and his father's entailed properties. This proved to be a protracted business, guaranteed to keep him out of mischief, and still incomplete at the time of his death in 1455. One of the principal obstacles was his mother, who, after Hotspur's death, married Thomas, Lord Camoys and retained her dower lands until her death in 1417. The properties involved were not large and recovery was straightforward. Not so with the estate that had been granted by Henry IV to his third son, Prince John, Duke of Bedford, since he did not die until 1435 and while he lived was far too powerful to be dispossessed. It took much litigation and an Act of Parliament after Bedford's death before the bulk of the properties were recovered. In the end, the Second Earl regained all the Percy properties in Northumberland, Yorkshire, Cumberland and Sussex and lost only six manors: three in Lincolnshire, two in Durham and one in Essex.

Throughout his life, the Second Earl assiduously pursued his claims to his family's property. In that respect, he was at one with his ancestors. In contrast to them, he appears not to have harboured the extreme political ambitions that drove his father and grandfather. As he entered middle age, the political discontents and rivalries that were to result in the forty-year period of upheaval known as the Wars of the Roses were beginning. In these years of strife, he and his two successors remained staunch supporters of Henry of Bolingbroke's descendants. He and his son both died in battle, fighting for Bolingbroke's grandson, Henry VI, while his grandson, the Fourth Earl of Northumberland, betrayed Richard III at Bosworth in 1485 and in doing so helped to ensure the Lancastrian restoration in the person of Henry VII. In curious contrast, the role of kingmaker was assumed by Richard Neville, Earl of Warwick, grandson of Ralph Neville, Earl of Westmorland. While the Percys had put Bolingbroke on the throne, Neville helped to replace his grandson in favour of the Mortimer claimant.

Glossary

Affinity: in the late fourteenth century, the king and the great nobility had 'affinities'. An affinity comprised a body of men, 'retainers', who were bound to their lord in some way and for some purpose. The composition of an affinity was varied, but it would normally include the leading members of the lord's household and his estate administration; and also an indefinite number of lesser landowners whom he wished to attach to him. The normal means of attachment was the 'indenture of retinue', in effect a contract that set out the mutual obligations of the two parties and the annual remuneration to be paid by the lord to the retainer. In most instances, the contract was for the life of the retainer and in peace and in war. The affinity clearly served a variety of normal, peaceful purposes, but it also contained a 'retinue' of men, who would form the nucleus of their lord's fighting force, should he go to war. It was also normal for at least some members of an affinity to wear a distinguishing badge or a 'livery', that is, a uniform.

Annuity: an annual sum of money assigned to a named individual or corporation, usually from the profits arising from a specified source. Annuities were also used instead of 'indentures of retainer' as a looser means of attaching one man to another.

Banneret: a knight of superior wealth and military competence, who raised and commanded a force of knights, men at arms and archers, normally amounting to forty or more men. A banneret's status was proclaimed by a banner, square or oblong in shape, bearing his personal arms. This banner clearly differed from that of an ordinary knight, which was in the form of a pennon with triangular tails.

Barony: the Crown created baronies for its leading supporters in the eighty years after the Conquest. There was no rule as to size, and many comprised the estates of pre-Conquest English thanes. The distinguishing characteristic of a barony was the enhanced judicial rights possessed by its holder over those living in its territory. Strictly, a barony could not be divided, although the land belonging to it could be.

Berewick: a discrete farm, originally for growing bere (barley).

Bondlands: held by bondmen, these were the core farming tenements of northern townships, probably created during a massive restructuring of rural arrangements in the twelfth century. Most comprised either twenty-four or thirty acres of arable land, distributed through two or more open fields in (roughly) half-acre strips, known as rigs, together with rights in the township common. These arrangements remained largely undisturbed until the later fourteenth century. Bondmen held 'by custom of the manor' and had no rights in Common Law.

Borough: boroughs were distinct communities created by both the Crown and major landlords, both lay and ecclesiastic, normally in conjunction with their castles, cathedrals or monasteries. Their purpose was economic development, very much like modern trading estates. Within their defined areas, their inhabitants enjoyed advantageous trading privileges and low, fixed rents for their properties, usually known as burgages. All boroughs strove, with varying degrees of success, to acquire from their founders (usually by purchase) some measure of self-government.

Cadency: in heraldry, the rules of which were well developed by the late fourteenth century, close relations of those who possessed coats of arms might be granted the right to use the same arms, but with a distinguishing mark to indicate subordinate status.

Carucate: deriving from the Latin word *carruca* = plough. Originally, the word indicated notional annual capacity of a single plough and consequently there was no national standard size. In practice, the term was not used as a unit of area but of obligation.

Cornage: an ancient royal due based upon cattle, the origins of which are obscure but may go back to the tenth century. It survived the Conquest in most parts of northern England.

Demesne: comprised those properties a landlord chose to retain under his immediate control. He could either farm such land himself or let it to tenant farmers, from whom he could recover it, either at will or at the end of a lease, and whose rent he could vary.

Drengage: a pre-Conquest form of land tenure that survived the imposition of Norman rule in the north of England and southern Scotland. Most surviving drengages comprised a single township. Originally, drengs were supervisors on large estates, responsible for such matters as collecting rents from farming tenants and seeing that they performed their other obligations. After the Conquest, most drengages were converted into rent-paying tenancies.

Enfeoffment to use: a legal means of avoiding the expensive interlude between the death of a Crown tenant and the accession of his heir. By this device the tenant enfeoffed all his estate to two or more trusted friends or lawyers 'to his use' during his lifetime. In other words, although in strict legal terms the ownership of his estate was now transferred to others, they acted as his trustees, allowing him to enjoy all the fruits of it as before. The arrangement also allowed him to prescribe to whom the trustees should transfer the estate after his death.

Entail: landowners came to have the right to prescribe the future descent in perpetuity of their estates after their death. Its purpose was to protect the estate against the profligacy of a future generation or to ensure that it remained in the family. Entails did not affect the right of a widow to her dower, that is, to possess one-third of her husband's estate for the rest of her life.

Escheat: the right of a landlord of a freehold tenant to repossess the estate in certain circumstances, commonly failure to pay rent or meet other agreed obligations, and the failure of heirs. The estates of those convicted of serious crimes would escheat to the Crown. A tenant's estate also escheated to the grantor if the heir was under age and remained in the grantor's possession (and to his profit) until the heir came of age. This made the right of considerable value, especially when the heir was very young and his estate very large.

Esquire: the social rank below that of knight, implying the possession of a smaller estate and less wealth.

Feudal levy: when William the Conqueror parcelled out most of England among his followers, he imposed on each the service of a specified number of knights (heavy cavalry), that is, the obligation to turn out with his quota when summoned by the Crown. From an early date this was recognised as a cumbersome means of raising troops and the Crown came to prefer charging a money composition (scutage) in lieu of service. By the late fourteenth century, the idea of the summoning the feudal levy as the means of raising an army was completely outdated.

Inquest: the normal and widespread means of establishing the truth of a matter. It involved the summoning of twelve men who were considered to be in possession of the facts. They were then placed upon oath to answer truthfully the questions put to them about the matter to be decided.

Knight's fee: the land given to a knight for his support in return for which he was required to perform military service and attend the grantor's court. Knights' fees had no prescribed size and consequently there was considerable variation. Large estates were normally rated at more than one knight's fee and smaller properties often had an obligation of a fraction of a knight's fee. Originally, knights' fees were not hereditary, but rapidly became so, along with increasingly complex rules governing their inheritance.

Liege homage: in European feudal society, it was assumed that every member of the landowning class would be either a lord or vassal, or, indeed, both. Vassal status was entered into by the public ceremony of homage. It was accepted that a man could be the vassal of more than one lord; but this would be a problem if two of a vassal's lords were in conflict and both demanded his loyalty. Hence the notion of liege homage: the lord to whom this was given had superior right to the vassal's loyalty and service. The vassal's liege homage took precedence over all other acts of simple homage that he had given to other lords.

Manor: a manor could be large or small in area: it could be coincident with a village territory; but equally it could comprise only part of a village or, on the other hand, several villages or parts of villages. The lordship of a manor conferred not only ownership of land but also certain jurisdictional rights over those who dwelt on it.

Mark: a mark was two-thirds of a pound sterling, that is, 13s 4d (67p). It was not a coin but a currency of account.

Messuage: a land holding, normally in a rural setting, where it would comprise a farmstead to which was attached cultivated land in the village fields and rights in the common. The term is also applied to tenements in boroughs, although there the term 'burgage' was also used.

Poll tax: the poll tax was a novel means of raising revenue for the Crown, which provoked a violent reaction in the late fourteenth century, just as it did in the late twentieth century. It was levied three times: in 1377 at a standard rate of 4d per head on all males between the ages of twelve and sixty; in 1379, when it was graduated, the rates ranging from £10 from the Duke of Lancaster (the richest man in England) down to 4d from labourers; and in 1381, when it triggered the uprising known as the Peasants' Revolt.

Remainder: an aspect of the entail system of inheritance control. The creator of an entail could lay down that his estate should descend in order to a prescribed list of successors, with a remainder to a final person, if any of the original inheritors failed to produce heirs.

Retinue: see **Affinity**, above.

Serfdom: a serf (and his family) was regarded as part of the stock of a manor and as such could be sold with it, or off it, at the wish of the lord of the manor. Serfdom was more prevalent in some parts of the country than in others; and by the late fourteenth century was on the wane and in some areas had all but disappeared. Serfs were able to escape their condition by purchase (if the owner was willing) or, in the case of women, by marriage to a free man; and also by living undetected in a borough for a year and a day. In practice, many serfs freed themselves simply by absconding.

Sergeanty: a non-military feudal tenure. Sergeanties carried a variety of obligations of an administrative nature, which was often replaced by a money rent.

Socage: the basic form of freehold tenure, which in most cases carried no other obligation than the payment of a money rent.

Subsidy: a form of direct taxation that became firmly established in the early decades of the fourteenth century. It was based, not upon income, but upon the assessed value of certain items of moveable property. The tax became fixed at fractional rates, a fifteenth in rural areas and a tenth in boroughs. Until 1334, a fresh assessment was made on every occasion but, as the tax became frequent, these became burdensome, expensive and subject to corruption. Consequently, after 1334 assessments were discontinued and a fixed sum was attached to each community, thus turning it into a form of land tax. The advantage to the Crown was that the yield was known in advance: £38,170. The Crown could not levy the tax at will, but had to secure parliamentary approval, in particular that of the Commons.

Further Reading

Primary sources

Primary sources for the events of this period fall into two broad categories. The more restricted are the records made by the Crown, which have been published in calendared (abbreviated and translated) form. Those of relevance here are the calendars of the Close Rolls, Fine Rolls, Inquests *post mortem*, Inquests Miscellaneous and Patent Rolls. Also under this heading may be included the *De Controversia in Curia Militaris inter Ricardum de Scrope et Robertum Grosvenor, miltes,* edited by Sir H.N. Nicolas (London, 1832).

Much longer and much more varied are the chronicles written by contemporaries or near contemporaries, the majority in monasteries. Nineteen have been published. Most were written in Latin, but some published versions have English translations in parallel:

Bellaguet, M.L., ed., *Chroniques du religieux de Saint-Denys,* vol. I (Paris, 1839)
Clarke, M.V. and Galbraith, V.H., eds, *Dieulacres Chronicle, Bulletin of the John Rylands Library,* vol. 14 (1930)
—, *Kirkstall Chronicle 1355–1400, Bulletin of the John Rylands Library,* vol. 15 (1931)
Davies, J.S., ed., *Davies' Chronicle, Camden Society,* 1st ser. (1856)
Ellis, H.F., ed., *Chronicle of John Hardyng* (London, 1812)
Galbraith, V.H., ed., *Anonimalle Chronicle 1333 to 1381* (Manchester, 1927)
Given Wilson, C., ed., *Chronicle of Adam Usk 1377–1421* (Oxford, 1997)
Hartshorne, C.H., *Cronica Monasterii de Alnewyke,* in *Feudal and Military Antiquities of Northumberland and the Scottish Border,* vol. II (Newcastle upon Tyne, 1858)
Haydon, F.S., ed., *Eulogium Historiarum sive Temporis* (Rolls Series) (London, 1863)
Hector, L.C. and Harvey, B.F., eds, *Westminster Chronicle 1381–1394* (Oxford, 1982)
Kingsford, C.L., *A Northern Chronicle 1399–1430,* in *English Historical Literature of the Fifteenth Century* (London, 1913)
—, 'The First Version of Hardyng's Chronicle', *English Historical Review,* vol. 27 (1912)
Martin, G.H., ed., *Knighton's Chronicle 1337–1396* (Oxford, 1995)

Riley, H.T., ed., *Annales Ricardi Secundi et Henrici Quarti,* (Rolls Series) (London, 1866)

Sayles, G.O., ed., *The Deposition of Richard II: Three Lancastrian Chronicles, Bulletin of the Institute of Historical Research,* vol. 54 (1981)

Scott, A.B. and Watt, D.E.R., eds, *Scotichronicon of Walter Bower,* vol. 7 (Aberdeen, 1996)

Stow, G.B., ed., *Historia Vitae et Regni Ricardi Secundi* (Philadelphia, 1977)

Thompson, E.M., ed., *Chronicon Angliae 1328–1388* (Rolls Series) (London, 1874)

Webb, J. ed., *Histoire du roy d'Angleterre Richart, traitant particulierement la rebellion de ses subjectz par Jean Creton, Archaeologia,* vol. 20 (1984)

Williams, B.W., ed., *Chronique de la Traison et Mort de Richart Deux, roy Dengleterre* (London, 1846).

In addition, there are selected documents in translation in:

Dobson, R.B., *The Peasants' Revolt of 1381,* 2nd edn (London, 1981)

Given Wilson, C., *Chronicles of the Revolution 1397–1400* (Manchester, 1993).

Primary sources specific to the Percy family are to be found in:

Inquisitiones Post Mortem for the First and Second Lords Percy, in Hartshorne, C.H., *Feudal and Military Antiquities of Northumberland and the Scottish Border,* vol. II (Newcastle upon Tyne, 1858)

Clough, M., ed., *Two Fitzalan Surveys, Sussex Record Society,* vol. 67 (1969)

Fonblanque, E. de B., *Annals of the House of Percy,* vol. I (London, 1887)

Martin, M.T, ed., *Percy Cartulary, Surtees Society,* vol. 117 (1911).

The extent of the problem of interpreting medieval chronicles is revealed by the existence of the numerous works designed to assist this process:

Duls, D.L., *Richard II in the early Chronicles* (The Hague, 1975)

Gransden, A.G., *Historical Writing in England II: c.1307 to the Early Sixteenth Century* (London, 1982)

Hansen, H.M., 'The Peasants' Revolt of 1381 and the Chronicles', *Journal of Medieval History,* vol. 6 (1980)

Martin, G.H., 'Narrative Sources for the Reign of Richard II', in Gillespie, J.L., *The Age of Richard II* (Stroud, 1997)

Palmer, J.J.N., 'The Authorship, Date and Historical Value of the French Chronicles of the Lancastrian Revolution', *Bulletin of the John Rylands Library,* vol. 61 (1978–79)

Stow, G.B., 'Richard II and Thomas Walsingham's Chronicles', *Speculum,* vol. 59 (1984)

—, 'Richard II in Jean Froissart's *Chroniques*', *Journal of Medieval History*, vol. 11 (1985)

Taylor, J., *English Historical Literature in the Fourteenth Century* (Oxford, 1987)

—, 'Richard II in the Chronicles', in Goodman, A., and Gillespie, J.L., *Richard II: The Art of Kingship* (Oxford, 1999)

Secondary sources

Armitage Smith, S., *John of Gaunt* (London, 1904)

Arnold, U., 'Eight Hundred Years of the Teutonic Order', in Barber, M., *The Military Orders* (Aldershot, 1994)

Arvanigian, M., 'Henry IV, the Northern Nobility and the Consolidation of the Regime', in Dodd, G., and Biggs, D., *Henry IV: The Establishment of the Regime, 1399–1406* (Woodbridge, 2003)

Aston, M., *Thomas Arundel: A Study of Church Life in the Reign of Richard II* (Oxford, 1967)

—, *Lollards and Reformers* (London, 1984)

Ayton, A., *Knights and Warhorses: Military Service and the English Aristocracy under Edward III* (Woodbridge, 1994)

—, 'English Armies in the Fourteenth Century', in Curry, A., and Hughes M., *Arms, Armies and Fortifications in the Hundred Years War* (Woodbridge, 1994)

Barber, M., 'John Norbury c. 1350–1414: An Esquire of Henry IV', *English Historical Review*, vol. 68 (1953)

Barber, R., *Edward, Prince of Wales and Aquitaine* (Woodbridge, 1978)

Barker, J.R.V., *The Tournament in England 1100–1400* (Woodbridge, 1986)

Barron, C.M., 'The Deposition of Richard II', in Taylor, J., and Childs, W., *Politics and Crisis in Fourteenth-Century England* (Stroud, 1990)

—, 'Richard II and London', in Goodman, A., and Gillespie, J.L., *Richard II: The Art of Kingship* (Oxford, 1999)

Bates, C.J., 'The Barony and Castle of Langley', *Archaeologia Aeliana*, 2nd ser., vol. 10 (1885)

Bean, J.W.M., 'The Percies' Acquisition of Alnwick', *Archaeologia Aeliana*, 4th ser., vol. 32 (1954)

—, 'The Percies and their Estates in Scotland', *Archaeologia Aeliana*, 4th ser., vol. 35 (1957)

—, *The Estates of the Percy Family, 1416–1537* (Cambridge, 1958)

—, 'Henry IV and the Percies', *History*, vol. 44 (1959)

—, *From Lord to Patron: Lordship in Late Medieval England* (Manchester, 1989)

Bellamy, J.G., 'The Northern Rebellions in the later years of Richard II', *Bulletin of the John Rylands Library*, vol. 47 (1964–65)

Bennett, M. 'The Development of Battle Tactics in the Hundred Years War', in Curry, A., and Hughes, M., *Arms, Armies and Fortifications in the Hundred Years War* (Woodbridge, 1994)

—, *Richard II and the Revolution of 1399* (Stroud, 1999)

—, 'Richard II and the Wider Realm', in Goodman, A., and Gillespie, J.L., *Richard II: The Art of Kingship* (Oxford, 1997)

171

—, 'Henry of Bolingbroke and the Revolution of 1399', in Dodd, G., and Biggs, D., *Henry IV: The Establishment of the Regime, 1399–1406* (Woodbridge, 2003)

Biggs, D., ' "A Wrong Conscience and Kindred bid me right": A reassessment of Edmund of Langley, Duke of York, and the Usurpation of Henry IV', *Albion*, vol. 26 (1994)

—, 'The Reign of Henry IV', in Saul, N., *Fourteenth-Century England* (Woodbridge, 2000)

Bilson, J., and Collier, C.V., 'Wressle Castle', *Yorkshire Archaeological Journal*, vol. 22 (1922)

Boardman, S.I., *The Early Stewart Kings: Robert II and Robert III, 1371–1406* (East Linton, 1996)

Bothwell, J.S., ed., *The Age of Edward III* (York, 2001)

Brown, A.L., 'The Reign of Henry IV', in Chrimes, S.B., Ross, C.D. and Griffiths, R.A., *Fifteenth-Century England, 1399–1509* (Manchester, 1972)

—, 'The English Campaign in Scotland, 1400', in Hearder, H., and Loyn, H.R., *British Government and Administration* (Cardiff, 1974)

Brown, M.H., 'The Development of Scottish Border Lordship, 1332–58', *Historical Research*, vol. 70 (1997)

Burne, A.H., *The Battlefields of England*, vols I (London, 1950) and II (London, 1952)

Childs, W.R., 'Anglo–Portuguese Relations in the Fourteenth Century', in Gillespie, J.L., *The Age of Richard II* (Stroud, 1997)

Clark, L., ed., *Authority and Subversion* (Woodbridge, 2003)

Cockayne, G.E. (with revisions by Gibbs, V. *et al.*), *The Complete Peerage of England, Scotland, Ireland, Great Britain and the United Kingdom* (London, 1887–98 and 1910–59)

Collins, S.M., 'The Blue Lion of Percy', *Archaeologia Aeliana*, 4th ser., vol. 24 (1946)

Curry, A., *The Hundred Years War* (London, 1993)

Dahmus, J., *William Courtney, Archbishop of Canterbury 1381–1396* (London, 1996)

Dalton, P., *Conquest, Anarchy and Lordship: Yorkshire 1066–1154* (Cambridge, 1994)

Davies, R.R., 'Richard II and the Principality of Chester, 1397–9', in DuBoulay, F.R.H., and Barron, C.M., *The Reign of Richard II* (London, 1971)

—, *Conquest, Co-existence and Change: Wales 1063–1415* (Oxford, 1987)

—, *The Revolt of Owain Glyn Dŵr* (Oxford, 1995)

—, *The First English Empire: Power and Identities in the British Isles, 1093–1543* (Oxford, 2000)

Dillon, H.A., 'Calais and its Pale', *Archaeologia*, vol. 53 (1893)

Dobson, R.B., 'The Risings in York, Beverley and Scarborough, 1380–81', in Hilton, R.H., and Aston, T.H., *The English Rising of 1381* (London, 1984)

DuBoulay, F.R.H., 'Henry of Derby's Expeditions to Prussia, 1390–1 and 1392', in DuBoulay, F.R.H., and Barron, C.M., *The Reign of Richard II* (London, 1971)

Dunn, A., 'Richard II and the Mortimer Inheritance', in Given Wilson, C., *The Fourteenth Century II* (London, 2002)

—, *The Great Rising of 1381* (Stroud, 2002)

—, 'Henry IV and the Politics of Resistance in Early Lancastrian England, 1399–1413', in Clark, L. ,ed., *The Fifteenth Century III: Authority and Subversion* (London, 2003)

Favier, J., *La Guerre de Cent Ans* (Paris, 1980)

Fletcher, W.G.D., 'Some Documents Relative to the Battle of Shrewsbury', *Transactions of the Shropshire Archaeological and Natural History Society*, 2nd ser., vol. 10 (1898)

Fonblanque, E.B. de, *Annals of the House of Percy*, vol. I (London, 1887)

Frame, R., *The Political Development of the British Isles 1100–1400* (Oxford, 1990)

Fraser, C.M., 'Some Durham Documents relating to the Hilary Parliament of 1404', *Bulletin of the Institute of Historical Research*, vol. 54 (1961)

Gillespie, J.L., 'Richard II's Archers of the Crown', *Journal of British Studies*, vol. 18 (1978–79)

—, 'Richard II's Knights: Chivalry and Patronage', *Journal of Medieval History*, vol. 13 (1987)

—, 'Richard II: Chivalry and Kingship', in Gillespie, J.L. (ed.), *The Age of Richard II* (Stroud, 1997)

—, 'Richard II: King of Battles?', in Gillespie, J.L. (ed.), *The Age of Richard II* (Stroud, 1997)

Given Wilson, C., *The Royal Household and the King's Affinity: Service, Politics and Finance, 1369–1413* (New Haven and London, 1986)

—, *The English Nobility in the Later Middle Ages* (London, 1989)

—, 'The manner of King Richard's renunciation: a Lancastrian narrative?' *English Historical Review*, vol. 108 (1993)

—, 'Richard II, Edward II and the Lancastrian Inheritance', *English Historical Review*, vol. 109 (1994)

—, 'Richard II and the Higher Nobility', in Goodman, A., and Gillespie, J.L., *Richard II: The Art of Kingship* (Oxford, 1999)

Goodman, A., *The Loyal Conspiracy: The Lords Appellant under Richard II* (London, 1971)

—, *John of Gaunt* (London, 1992)

—, and Tuck, A., *War and Border Societies in the Middle Ages* (London, 1992)

—, and Gillespie, J.L., *Richard II: The Art of Kingship* (Oxford, 1997)

Hay, D., 'The Division of the Spoils of War in Fourteenth-Century England', *Transactions of the Royal Historical Society*, 5th ser., vol. 4 (1954)

Hedley, W.P., *Northumberland Families*, vol. I (1968)

Henneman, J.B., *Olivier de Clisson and Political Society in France under Charles V and Charles VI* (Philadelphia, 1996)

—, 'France in the Middle Ages', in Bonney, R. (ed), *The Rise of the Fiscal State in Europe* (Oxford, 1999)

Hicks, M.A., *Bastard Feudalism* (London, 1995)

Holmes, G.A., *The Good Parliament* (Oxford, 1973)

Housley, N., 'The Bishop of Norwich's Crusade, May 1383', *History Today*, vol. 33 (1983)

Johnston, D.B., 'The Interim Years: Richard II and Ireland 1395–1399', in Lydon, J.E., *England and Ireland in the Later Middle Ages* (Dublin, 1973)

—, 'Richard II and Gaelic Ireland', *Irish Historical Studies*, vol. 22 (1980)

—, 'Richard II's departure from Ireland, July 1399', *English Historical Review*, vol. 98 (1983)

Jones, M.C.E.J., *Ducal Brittany* (Oxford, 1970)

Jones, R.H., *The Royal Policy of Richard II: Absolutism in the Later Middle Ages* (London, 1968)

Keen, M.H., *The Laws of War in the Middle Ages* (London, 1965)

—, *Nobles, Knights and Men at Arms in the Middle Ages* (London, 1996)

King, A., 'They have the Hertes of the People by North: Northumberland, the Percies and Henry IV, 1399–1408', in Dodd, G., and Biggs, D., *Henry IV: The Establishment of the Regime, 1399–1406* (Woodbridge, 2003)

Kirby, J.L., 'Calais sous les Anglais 1399–1413', *Revue du Nord*, vol. 37 (1955)

—, *Henry IV of England* (London, 1970)

Labarge, M.W., *Gascony, England's First Colony 1204–1453* (1980)

LePatourel, J., 'L'Occupation Anglaise de Calais au XIVe Siecle', *Revue du Nord*, vol. 33 (1951)

Lewis, N.B., 'The Last Feudal Summons of the English Feudal Levy, 13th June 1385', *English Historical Review*, vol. 73 (1958)

Lindenbaum, S., 'The Smithfield Tournament of 1390', *Journal of Medieval and Renaissance Studies*, vol. 20 (1990)

Lodge, E.C., *Gascony under English Rule* (London, 1929)

Lomas, R.A., *A Power in the Land: The Percys* (East Linton, 1999)

Macdonald, A.J., *Border Bloodshed: Scotland and England at War 1369–1403* (East Linton, 2000)

McKisack, M., *The Fourteenth Century* (Oxford, 1959)

McNiven, P., 'The Cheshire Rising of 1400', *Bulletin of the John Rylands Library*, vol. 52 (1969–70)

—, 'The Betrayal of Archbishop Scrope', *Bulletin of the John Rylands Library*, vol. 54 (1971–72)

—, 'The Scottish Policy of the Percies and the Strategy of the Rebellion of 1403', *Bulletin of the John Rylands Library*, vol. 62 (1979–80)

—, 'The Men of Cheshire and the Rebellion of 1403', *Transactions of the History Society of Lancashire and Cheshire*, vol. 129 (1980)

—, 'Legitimacy and Consent: Henry IV and the Lancastrian Title, 1399–1406', *Medieval Studies*, vol. 44 (1982)

—, 'Rebellion, Sedition and the Legend of Richard II's Survival in the Reigns of Henry IV and Henry V', *Bulletin of the John Rylands Library*, vol. 76 (1994)

Mathew, G., *The Court of Richard II* (London, 1968)

Melia, S., 'The Battle of Homildon Hill', *Northern Archaeology*, vols 15–16 (1998)

Meyrick, S.M., 'Account of the Tomb of Sir John Chandos', *Archaeologia*, vol. 20 (1824)

Morgan, P., *War and Society in Medieval Cheshire*, (London, 1987)

—, 'Henry IV and the shadow of Richard II', in Archer, R.E., ed., *Crown, Government and People in the Fifteenth Century* (Stroud, 1995)

Mott, R.A.K., 'Richard II and the Crisis of 1397', in Wood, I., and Loud, G.A., *Church and Chronicle in the Middle Ages* (1991)

Myers, J.N.L., 'The Campaign of Radcot Bridge', *English Historical Review*, vol. 42 (1927)

Neville, C.J., *Violence, Custom and the Law: the Anglo–Scottish Borderlands in the Later Middle Ages* (Edinburgh, 1998)

—, 'Scotland, the Percies and the Law in 1400', in Dodd, G., and Biggs, D., *Henry IV: The Establishment of the Regime, 1399–1406* (Woodbridge, 2003)

Nicholson, R., *Scotland: The Later Middle Ages* (Edinburgh, 1974)

Northumberland County History, 15 vols (Newcastle upon Tyne, 1893–1940)

Orme, N., *From Childhood to Chivalry: The Education of English Kings and Aristocracy 1066–1530* (London, 1984)

Ormrod, M.W., *The Reign of Edward III: The Crown and Political Society in England, 1327–1377* (New Haven and London, 1990)

—, 'England in the Middle Ages', in Bonney, R. (ed.), *The Rise of the Fiscal State in Europe* (Oxford, 1999)

Palmer, J.J.N., 'England and the Great Schism 1388–1399', *English Historical Review*, vol. 83 (1968)

—, 'The Impeachment of Michael de la Pole in 1386' *Bulletin of the Institute of Historical Research*, vol. 42 (1969)

—, 'The Parliament of 1385 and the Constitutional Crisis of 1386', *Speculum*, vol. 46 (1971)

—, *England, France and Christendom, 1377–1399* (London, 1972)

—, 'England, France and the Flemish Succession 1361–1369', *Journal of Medieval History*, vol. 2 (1976)

Philpotts, C.J., 'John of Gaunt and English Policy towards France 1389–95', *Journal of Medieval History*, vol. 16 (1990)

Plucknet, T.F.T., 'State Trials under Richard II', *Transactions of the Royal Historical Society*, 5th ser., vol. 2 (1952)

Prestwich, M., *The Three Edwards: War and State in England 1272–1377* (London, 1980)

Priestley, E.J., *The Battle of Shrewsbury, 1403* (Shrewsbury, 1979)

Ramsey, J.H., *Genesis of Lancaster 1303–1399*, 2 vols (Oxford, 1913)

Reeves, A.C., *The Marcher Lords of Wales* (Llandybie, 1983)

Reid, R.R., 'The Office of Warden of the Marches; its Origin and Early History', *English Historical Review*, vol. 32 (1917)

Reitemeier, A., 'Born to be a Tyrant? The Childhood and Education of Richard II', in Given Wilson, C., *The Fourteenth Century II* (London, 2002)

Reville, A., *Le Soulevement des Travailleurs D'Angleterre en 1381* (Paris, 1898)

Robertson, E.C., 'On the skeletons exhumed at Elsdon and their probable connection with the Battle of Otterburn', *History of the Berwickshire Naturalists Club*, vol. 9 (1882)

Rogers, A., 'The Political Crisis of 1401', *Nottingham Medieval Studies*, vol. 12 (1968)

Rogers, C.J., *War Cruel and Sharp: English Strategy under Edward III, 1327–1360* (Woodbridge, 2000)

Roskell, J.S., *The Impeachment of Michael de la Pole, Earl of Suffolk in 1386* (Manchester, 1984)

Ross, C.D., 'Forfeiture for Treason in the Reign of Richard II', *English Historical Review*, vol. 71 (1956)

Rosser, G., *Medieval Westminster* (Oxford, 1989)

Russell, P.E., *The English Intervention in Spain and Portugal in the Time of Edward III and Richard II* (Oxford, 1955)

Saul, N., 'Richard II and the Vocabulary of Kingship', *English Historical Review*, vol. 110 (1995)
—, *Richard II* (New Haven and London, 1997)
Sayles, G.O., 'Richard II in 1381 and 1397', *English Historical Review*, vol. 94 (1979)
Seward, D., *The Monks of War* (London, 1972)
Sherborne, J.W., 'Indentured Retainers and English Expeditions to France, 1369–1381', *English Historical Review*, vol. 79 (1964)
—, 'The English Navy, Shipping and Manpower 1369–1389', *Past and Present*, vol. 37 (1967)
—, 'The Battle of La Rochelle and the War at Sea 1372–5', *Bulletin of the Institute of Historical Research*, vol. 42 (1969)
—, 'Richard II's Return to Wales', *Welsh History Review*, vol. 7 (1974–75)
—, 'Perjury and the Lancastrian Revolution of 1399', in Sherborne, J.W., *War, Politics and Culture in the Fourteenth Century* (London, 1994)
Somerville, R., *History of the Duchy of Lancaster*, vol. I (London, 1975)
Stamp, A.E., 'Richard II and the Death of the Duke of Gloucester', *English Historical Review*, vol. 38 (1934)
Steel, A., *Richard II* (Cambridge, 1941)
Storey, R.L., 'The Wardens of the Marches of England towards Scotland, 1377–1489', *English Historical Review*, vol. 72 (1957)
Tait, J.S., 'Did Richard II Murder the Duke of Gloucester?', in Tout, T.F., and Tait, J.S., *Historical Essays by Members of Owens College* (Manchester, 1902)
Tate, G., *History of Alnwick*, 2 vols (Alnwick, 1866–69)
Taylor, C., 'Edward III and the Plantagenet Claim to the French Throne', in Bothwell, J. S., *The Age of Edward III* (York, 2001)
Thompson, J.A.F., *The Transformation of Medieval England 1370–1529* (London, 1983)
Tuck, A., 'Richard II and the Border Magnates', *Northern History*, vol. 3 (1968)
—, 'The Cambridge Parliament, 1388', *English Historical Review*, vol. 4 (1969)
—, 'Northumbrian Society in the Fourteenth Century', *Northern History*, vol. 6 (1971)
—, *Richard II and the English Nobility* (London, 1973)
—, 'War and Society in the Medieval North', *Northern History*, vol. 21 (1985)
—, 'The Emergence of a Northern Nobility', *Northern History*, vol. 22 (1986)
—, 'Richard II and the Hundred Years War', in Taylor, J., and Childs, W., *Politics and Crises in Fourteenth Century England* (Stroud, 1990)
—, *Crown and Nobility: England 1272–1461*, 2nd ed. (London, 1999)
Vale, J., *Edward III and Chivalry* (Woodbridge, 1982)
Vale, M.G.A., *English Gascony 1379–1453* (Oxford, 1970)
—, *The Angevin Legacy and the Hundred Years War 1250–1340* (Oxford, 1990)
Victoria County History of Shropshire, vol. II (London, 1973)
Vine, M.J., 'Two Yorkshire Rebels: Peter de Brus and Richard de Percy', *Yorkshire Archaeological Journal*, vol. 47 (1975)
Walker, S., *The Lancastrian Affinity 1361–1389* (Oxford, 1990)
—, 'The Yorkshire Risings of 1405: Texts and Contexts', in Dodd, G., and Biggs, D., *Henry IV: The Establishnent of the Regime, 1399–1406* (Woodbridge, 2003)
Wallon, H.A., *Richard II*, 2 vols (Paris, 1864)

Further Reading

Watt, J.A., 'The Anglo–Irish Colony under Strain', in Cosgrove, A., *A New History of Ireland*, vol. II (Dublin, 1987)

Waugh, S.L., *England in the Reign of Edward III* (Cambridge, 1991)

Whelan, W., *The History and Topography of Cumberland and Westmorland* (Pontefract, 1860)

White, R., *History of the Battle of Otterburn fought in 1388* (Newcastle upon Tyne, 1857)

Wright, H.G., 'The Protestation of Richard II in the Tower in September 1399', *Bulletin of the John Rylands Library*, vol. 23 (1939)

Wylie, J.H., *History of England under Henry IV*, vols I (1884), II (1894) and III (1895)

Index

*The names Lescrope and Scrope, both of which were used by contemporaries, refer to the same family.

179